MAUI'S MITTEE AND
THE GENERAL

MAUI'S MITTEE AND THE GENERAL

A glimpse into the lives of Mr. and Mrs. Frank Fowler Baldwin

Irma Gerner Burns

Ku Pa'a Incorporated
Honolulu, Hawaii

First Edition
1991

Library of Congress Cataloging in Publication Data Number applied for.

Typography by Unitype, Inc., Honolulu, Hawaii U.S.A.
Manufactured in United States of America

Designed by Martha F.M. Smith

ISBN: 0-914916-90-4 hardbound

Maui's Mittee And The General
Also includes extract from **A MEMOIR OF HENRY PERRINE BALDWIN** by Arthur D. Baldwin

Published by:

KU PA'A INCORPORATED
formerly Topgallant Publishing Co., Ltd.
Honolulu, Hawaii 96813

INTRODUCTION

Maui-born Irma Gerner Burns served as secretary to Frank Baldwin and companion to Mrs. Frank Baldwin for many years and shares her memories. Her family relates to 260 years of service in the sugar industry.

For John Castle Baldwin

"The ordinary man will take his history, in common with much else, largely on trust: and this for two reasons. He must begin to learn it long before he is equipped to question it; and thereafter, he may quite possibly remember or forget it without ever discovering the inclination, or the need, to examine the evidence for what was never allowed to seem in doubt. For history is the memory of mankind, and the desire to be remembered has more in common with ambition to be believed, than with a devotion to accuracy. After all, men do not remember and record things because they are true but because they are memorable."

J. J. Coulton

"The Chronicler of European Chivalry"

CONTENTS

Harriet Kittredge   Frank Baldwin
1900

MITTEE AND THE GENERAL

Mittee: The woman who was to become Mittee Baldwin was the granddaughter of Joseph Greenough Kittredge and the former Harriet Worcester; New Englanders who moved to San Francisco with their son, Edward Henry, in 1850. Edward grew to become an astute businessman and investor. At the time of his marriage to Mary Caroline Johnson, daughter of a sea captain, in 1871, he owned a thriving lumber business; the California Door Company.

Mittee's older sister, Ethel Mary, was born on April 14, 1875. Mittee came along on January 24, 1879. Perhaps because a son had been hoped for, the child remained unnamed and answered informally to "Baby" for several years. Then on a visit to her grandparents, while touring the stables with her grandfather he suddenly announced, "Your name shall be Harriet," (her grandmother's name). This is a poignant family recollection, because Joseph Kittredge died suddenly on the following day.

Father Edward was a man of strong persuasions. He did not believe in celebrating birthdays, maintaining that age was not a significant entry in the log of life. Nevertheless family birth dates were known to the children. Ethel unwittingly disturbed her father one year by hoarding her allowance to purchase two expensive books she knew he wanted, which she presented to him at the dinner table. He put the wrapped gift aside unopened, and reminded her that birthdays were not to be remembered in his house. Ethel left the table weeping, but Harriet followed her father's injunction throughout her life.

In her teens, Harriet was sent to school in Switzerland, where her inability to speak the language made her a lonely and unhappy young lady. She prevailed upon her parents to transfer her to a boarding school in Oakland, California. Sometime during her sojourn there, her mother took her sister Ethel to Venice.

Mary Kittredge's sister "Sadie" had married a Frenchman who was barrister to King George and they resided in London. Aunt Sadie became a close friend to Queen Mary, and the queen invited Sadie's nieces to come to London and present themselves at Court. In preparation for this occasion the young ladies were instructed in royal protocol. Beautiful long-trained gowns were made for them which were complimented with long white gloves and diamond tiaras. The pomp and ceremony was dazzling, and the memory of that evening was treasured by Harriet and Ethel all their lives.

Upon their return to San Francisco, the sisters made their debut into society wearing the gowns they had worn when being presented to the King and Queen of England.

General: The man who would become known to his familiars as "General" and to all others on Maui as "The General" was christened Frank Fowler Baldwin. He was the fifth of eight children born to Henry Perrine and Emily Alexander Baldwin; born on March 30, 1878 at Sunnyside on Maui. His brothers were Harry, Arthur, William, Samuel and Fred, and his sisters; Charlotte, who married Harold W. Rice, and Maud, who married Joseph P. Cooke. On both sides of the family he was descended from missionary grandparents.

The nickname he was to bear for much of his life derived from his penchant for polo playing, and probably had much to do with his demeanor on the polo fields while playing the game with his three sons.

Frank Baldwin literally fell into Harriet's life from a bicycle; an old fashioned velocipede with a large front wheel and a small one in the rear. Harriet was on the front lawn of her boarding school, Miss Horton's School for Girls, in Oakland, California. Her attention was drawn to a young bicycler across the street, attempting futilely to escape from several pursuing children who successfully diverted his rear wheel, causing him to fall. Harriet naturally had to ascertain that he was unhurt. The first words from Frank that Harriet ever heard were directed at those errant children, and his language was not at all gentlemanly.

When finally he turned his attention to Harriet, the two were instantly attracted to each other. During the ensuing conversation, Harriet learned that he was from Hawaii, and boarded nearby with two spinsters while attending Oakland High School. Frank learned that Miss Horton's would be having a dance evening shortly, and in this manner the romance began.

But as the weeks passed, the burgeoning romance suffered a setback and had to be continued by correspondence. Frank's grades had fallen somewhat and his parents decided to transfer him clear across the continent to the Hotchkiss School in Lakeville, Connecticut.

Harriet continued to attend her proper, strict and genteel institution. Since even outgoing mail was scrutinized, Harriet had to resort surreptitiously to lowering her letters to Frank, tied with elastic, from

2

an upper story window for an accomplice below to mail. This co-conspirator was her life-long friend Helene Erdman, destined to marry Paul Fagan, who bought a ranch in Hana which is now known as the Hotel Hana Maui. Harriet was often a guest at the Erdman home on weekends.

Edward Kittredge's business and social schedule left very little time for him to enjoy his family. This prompted him to purchase a fruit ranch in Saratoga, California, which also served as a much needed retreat for himself. The family spent many enjoyable vacations on the ranch, and perhaps this is where Harriet's insatiable love of horses, riding and ranching surfaced.

Upon graduation from Miss Horton's, Harriet chose to go on to nursing school. She completed her training there, but decided that "emptying bedpans" was not meant to be her life's vocation.

Her parents had been aware for some time that Harriet was in love with Frank Baldwin. They had hoped she would marry a man named Carl Howard, whom she described as an "old man of 21." Alas, no other information concerning this young worthy has been obtainable.

When Mary Kittredge was at last convinced that her daughter's feeling for Frank was genuine and lasting, mother and daughter embarked on a visit to Frank's parents in the "Sandwich Islands," (a most desolate territory, Mrs. Kittredge insisted).

Mary Kittredge and Emily Baldwin had little in common. Mary was an elegant and sophisticated San Francisco socialite, who spent much thought and time on dress and grooming. Emily paid little attention to her attire. While she was certainly an attractive and intelligent woman, she was a plantation wife, and inculcated with the values of missionary antecedents.

The visit to the Baldwin home in Haiku was for only one week, but to Mary the time passed subjectively slowly. Plantation dust was abhorrent to her, and the social activities more limited than those to which she was accustomed. She remarked that there was not even a "cocktail hour." Her main activity was to take long walks with Harriet, often to the Maliko Gulch vineyard to pick grapes. There is little doubt that the long voyage home was welcome to Mary when finally the two women left Maui.

Edward Kittredge had not approved of his wife's island visit. It had been undertaken unnecessarily, he thought, to evaluate the Baldwins' suitability as prospective in-laws. That disapproval may have been why he was in New York on business when the women returned to San Francisco.

Frank graduated from Hotchkiss in 1896 and went on to Yale University. In 1898 he decided that what he wanted to be in life was a "dirt farmer" on Maui, and he set off for home.

Harriet & Frank: Harriet arrived home from nursing school one day to be told that a young man had telephoned and would call again. Frank had just arrived in San Francisco and wasted no time about proposing marriage. Harriet wasted no time about accepting, and the marriage took place on April 27, 1900, in the Congregational Church in Oakland, at "precisely" 4:54 pm. Witnesses to the wedding were her father and Frank's uncle Samuel T. Alexander. Frank was then 23 years of age, and Harriet, 21. It was said to have been a lovely wedding.

After the wedding, Harriet's father gave her two hundred dollars and advised her that from then on, " . . . the key would be on the outside of the door."

The couple honeymooned in New York.

Maui: Ethel Baldwin, wife to Frank's brother Harry, often recollected that Harriet was the most beautiful bride ever to come to Maui. There is no evidence that she had any difficulty adjusting to territorial Hawaii, or that she missed the urbanity of San Francisco. She settled easily and happily into her first Hawaiian home, which was located just above Makawao Union Church in Paia. (There were to be sixteen other residences subsequently.) She had always made friends easily, and Frank had numerous congenial relatives. On Sundays the couple attended Congregational services at Makawao Union Church, after which many of the Baldwin clan would gather for dinner at the Maluhia home of H.P. Baldwin on Olinda Road.

The newlyweds were fortunate in obtaining the services of T. Ah Fook, an expert in the culinary arts. He also tended to the chickens and cared for Frank's work horse, who was an inveterate rover. Mittee loved to relate that on many a morning back in those days, there would come a knocking at the bedroom door, and a plaintive, "Mista Baldwin, horsey no moah." And Frank would have to arise and dress and go off with Ah Fook to find the errant creature. In later years Ah Fook opened a small grocery store which grew into today's "Ah Fook Supermarket" in the Kahului Shopping Mall.

Frank's first employment, from which he gained much practical experience, was with the Paia Plantation. Even as a neophyte he had five men working under him. His salary was $150.00 per month, and $25.00 of that went to pay their cook. Plantation living entailed certain obligations and amenities. Harriet could not manage on so little money and finally applied to her father, who supplemented their income to a modest extent.

In 1902 Frank was transferred to the Hawaiian Commercial and Sugar Company (HC&S) as division overseer. This necessitated moving to Spreckelsville, just across the street from the old Spreckelsville Store.

This was the same year the HC&S Puunene mill was completed. Frank's father Henry Perrine, plantation manager, chose to name the mill after a cinder cone in the region, and the whole area adopted the name and bears it still. The word "Puunene" derives from "puu," Hawaiian for hill, and "nene," goose. The cinders from that cone are long gone, having been used for road and airport construction, and the "goose" derivative is inexplicable altogether. As far as this writer can ascertain, geese never entered the area until 1951, when 500 day-old goslings were brought to HC&S to implement a weed-killing experiment. The little barn housing the goslings was appropriately named "Hale Nene" (house of geese). When the weedeaters failed their mission they were turned into tempting table morsels.

Frank was appointed manager of HC&S Co four years later, and two years after he assumed that position (1908), company directors voted to thank him for his ". . . able, efficient and satisfactory" manner of management, and instructed Alexander and Baldwin (A&B) to buy him a ". . . first class automobile."

The first automobile ever on Maui belonged to Frank's father. J.B. Castle, a partner in the firm of Alexander & Baldwin, was commissioned to make the purchase for him while on a business trip to the Mainland. After reaching San Francisco, Mr. Castle received a letter from Henry containing the following instructions:

> "Now in regard to the horseless carriage you are going to buy for me. It would be well to write them that some of our grades up and down gulches are as high as 10%, and that I will want brakes on the wheels."

The machine never did run away with Henry on the grades, but evidently it gave considerable mechanical trouble, as it is remembered as ". . . every week fix 'em."

Family: In spite of Harriet's avowed intention never to have children, her first son was born on May 10, 1903 and named Edward Henry Kittredge, after her father. He grew to be tall and very handsome; a bit of a cowboy who loved ranch life. Harriet miscarried another male child, and then bore two more sons. Asa Fred was born on November 17, 1906, and was named Asa for a very dear friend in New York and for his Uncle Fred who had died a year earlier. He, too, grew to be tall and handsome; a bit reserved, a warm and generous man. Lawrence Alexander was born on January 7, 1909. "Chu," as everyone called him, grew up to be the most popular of the sons, well-loved by all who knew him.

Edward was born in Paia, and the other two in Spreckelsville. The Spreckelsville Hospital, founded in 1885, was among the first plantation hospitals established in Hawaii. HC&S acquired their first resident physician in 1896, and two "lady nurses" from Philadelphia in 1900. It had the first x-ray machine in the Islands in 1903. Another hospital was opened in Paia in 1898 which functioned until 1909, when a new facility was built in upper Paia, below Makawao Union Church. The old hospital became the Paia Clubhouse for bachelors.

With three active boys to tend, Harriet now needed more help to manage her household. Yuki Kamemoto entered her employ and remained with the family for 35 years, until she returned to Japan in 1938.

Harriet's nickname, Mittee, began evolving when her sons were young. They loved for her to read stories to them, and were especially fond of an old English tale whose main character was named Mrs. Mittens, so "Mother" became " Mrs. Mittens." The transition to "Mittee" was completed many years later, when her son Edward's young son, Greg, was about three years old. His baby-talk produced "Mittee," and thenceforth she was Mittee to all.

Mittee idolized her boys and enjoyed being with them. They were taught to ride horses at an early age, and Mittee recalled them riding to Waihee with watermelons on their saddles, to be consumed there after the exertion of the ride. Sometimes she and the boys would pick up horses from Worth Aiken, a Paia businessman who rented horses for expeditions to the summit of Haleakala from his mountain home, Idlewild, at the top of the old Olinda Road. It would be a day-long round trip and at that altitude, cold and fatiguing. Under those circumstances, Mittee permitted the moderate use of "spirits," which warmed the boys up, but combined with the fatigue, contributed to making them so sleepy on the homeward ride that Mittee would dismount and lead their horses down the trail.

Shocking and saddening news from California interrupted this life of placid pleasures and mild alarms in 1916. Mittee's father learned that he had cancer and committed suicide. This strong man could not face a future of pain, dependency and hopelessness. Mary Kittredge outlived her husband by ten years.

The boys, each in turn, attended Maui Grammar School in Hamakuapoko; adjacent to the old Maui High School. It was then the only English Standard school on the Island. As Maui High grew to accommodate students from Central and East Maui, a new grammar school was built in Spreckelsville. (Kaunoa School, as it was called, today houses a senior citizen center.) The only requirement for enrollment in either grammar school was to pass an English Standard test. It was thought that only haoles (Caucasians) could attend these schools. That was not true, but the reality of the times was that immigrant children could not pass the English test, so the schools became in effect a haole preserve.

The Baldwin boys spent a year or two at Maui High, and then were sent, each in turn, to Thacher's School in Ojai, California, and went from there to colleges of their choice.

All the boys would come home for the Christmas holidays, because despite the shortness of the visit, this was a very special holiday on Maui. On Christmas and New Year's Eves, professional and amateur singers would "serenade" from house to house. Some households could spare a dollar for the singers, and some could spare ten. Many of the serenaders would earn a large percentage of their annual incomes on those two nights. Groups queued up waiting to perform. Frank was always well-stocked with ten and twenty-dollar bills, for the serenading continued into the early morning hours, with many good wishes for Mr. and Mrs. *"Paluina"* (Baldwin) as they were affectionately called by many of Maui's people.

Among the benefits derived from having Yuki Kamemoto living with the family was the children's exposure to the Japanese tongue. Chu, in particular, had a talent for the language, and chose to make a more thorough study of it. The principal of the Puunene Japanese Language School, Mr. Teiichiro Maehara, tutored him at home until he attained fluency, and then he went to Japan for further study. His mastery of Japanese was helpful to his career. He became, first Welfare Director, and then Personnel Director for HC&S Co. Able as he was to understand and communicate with Japanese old-timers, he grew to be one of the most popular supervisors on the plantation. His assistance was available not only at work; personnel were welcome in his home at any hour to discuss their problems.

When Henry Perrine Baldwin died in 1911, Frank became both Manager and President of HC&S. His father's diligent guidance had prepared him to assume the enormous responsibilities involved in running a large corporation, and under Frank's skilled direction, the

The General

plantation soon emerged as the leader in the industry.

From Spreckelsville, Mittee and Frank moved to a house built for them just above the old Puunene Hospital, which is chiefly remembered by the family for the terrific dust problems which plagued them whenever the fields surrounding the house were harvested. To combat this, wet cheesecloth was hung around the house, but that hardly deterred the harvesting dust. This nuisance probably was instrumental in Mittee's decision to build a home upcountry. She engaged the services of C.W. Dickey, Frank's cousin on his father's side and architect of many family dwellings on Maui.

Olinda: She wanted a New England style home, patterned on "The House of the Seven Gables." Dickey permitted only 5 gables, but designed a grandiose and gracious house containing large rooms and elegant staircases. The home was situated on Olinda Road, just below the H.P. Baldwin Maluhia manor. It was subsequently sold to Frank's brother-in-law Harold Rice who gave it to his son "Oskie" as a wedding gift. John Baldwin, Mittee's grandson, now owns and resides in this home. He has restored it to its original splendor, and it was recently awarded and registered a "historical place" in the annals of Hawaii's historical places by the State Historic Preservation Division of the Department of Land & Natural Resources.

Mittee's sister Ethel had married a man named George Baker, who died of a heart attack on a train while the couple were en route to a visit in the East. Some time later, she visited Maui and met the man who would be her future husband. Arthur Collins was a civil engineer who had been employed by Harry Baldwin to work in the East Maui ditch country. The family recollection is, that as a dinner guest in Mittee's new home, he beheld Ethel descending the staircase, and fell in love with her instantly. They were married in Boston in 1908, and returned to make their home on Maui. The couple had three children, Mary, Patricia and Walter; all Maui-born, and Mittee had her own kin close to her at last.

Sister Ethel was inadvertently responsible for an accident that cost her brother-in-law the little finger of his right hand. People often wondered how Frank got his "mumu" finger. One Sunday he helped the church-bound ladies into the automobile, as gentlemen used to do, and Ethel closed her door prematurely, severing the finger. Church forgotten, they rushed him to the hospital where doctors reattached the finger, but the graft did not take.

In 1914 the Kahakuloa Ranch, owned chiefly by Frank and managed by Angus McPhee was closed out as a ranch property and the

Olinda House

Mittee with sons Edward and Chu

6,000 acres were sub-leased to a number of smaller ranches in the area. No other information is available on this undertaking.

Lanai: Frank enjoyed many hunting trips on the island of Lanai. Roland Gay often told of the time that he was too busy to accompany Frank on a hunt. He equipped Frank with a horse and an excellent hunting dog and sent him off to get his prey. Later that morning Roland happened by his father's office and found the hunting dog lying by the door. He was puzzled as to what had happened. His father did not know, but about that time they saw Frank riding back at a gallop "swearing at the top of his lungs." He said: "I'm going to kill that dog." He finally calmed down, and the facts became known. The dog had pointed to birds three times and had given up and came back on his own.

Gay and Robinson had Lanai up for sale in 1917. Frank and his brother Harry formed a partnership and purchased it. These two brothers were very compatible, both being leaders in the sugar industry. Harry had come up the ladder from the Haiku Sugar Company to Paia Plantation Company, thence to managership of Maui Agricultural Company. Others were also interested in purchasing the island, including Jim Dole, but there was no water system or crop expertise established. The Baldwin boys paid $588,000 for the island which was bought for cattle purposes, and Roland Gay was retained to run the ranch. Frank and Harry then developed a water system by running a 20 mile pipeline from Maunalei Gulch around the northwest end of the island to the upland pastures and installed a water wheel that supplied the livestock water system with no fuel cost. In 1920 the Baldwin boys brought twelve deer from Molokai to Lanai at $50 a head to stimulate hunting.

Lanai was again up for sale in 1922. Frank was negotiating the purchase of Ulupalakua Ranch at the time and needed funds. He wanted his eldest son Edward to take over the management of the Ranch upon his graduation from college. Jim Dole took a long second look at pineapple for Palawai and the new water system and Dole's Hawaiian Pineapple Company paid $1,100,000 for the island. Frank and Harry each received approximately $500,000. Harry then leased the island of Kahoolawe and set up a fine ranch there.

Kulamanu: It is not known why Mittee wanted another home in the upcountry area. She engaged an architect, a Mr. Hitchcock of San Francisco to help her with the new endeavor. He was "the man that came to dinner" and stayed six months until the house was built. The area was called "Kulamanu" and Mittee and Frank enjoyed living on their fabulous 100-acre estate complete with stables, guest houses and living quarters for their help.

Mittee spent many hours at Kulamanu riding her favorite horse "Ukulele." As soon as the purchase of Ulupalakua Ranch was finalized, the home was sold (completely furnished) to George R. "Bobby" Carter, son of former Hawaii territorial governor. Bobby and Mittee were close friends, each enjoying the other's fabulous sense of humor.

Ulupalakua: In December of 1922 Mittee and Frank moved to their newly acquired Ulupalakua Ranch which consisted of an area of 22,000 acres plus a large leasehold of Territorial land. They occupied the beautiful big house built by the renowned Captain Makee in 1856. Makee had spent money lavishly at Ulupalakua and at that time it was the most beautiful estate in the Kingdom of Hawaii. However, the severe drought in the year 1877 resulted in the loss of much of the fine landscaping. Since Edward was still attending the University of Virginia, Angus MacPhee (a Wyoming cattleman) was retained to run the ranch.

Mittee loved Ulupalakua. In anticipation of Edward taking over the management of the Ranch, another home was built in the area a short distance away. This home was outfitted with a "live-it-up" room called "The Beer Parlor" for the boys and their guests to enjoy when they came home from school with their friends for summer vacations.

Nephews Manduke Baldwin and Oskie Rice spent many summers on the ranch. Often, early in the morning, Mittee would accompany all the boys on wild cattle hunts in the *paninis* (cactus), up and down Makena. On one trip down the Makena pastures, she was charged by a wild bull which the boys were attempting to catch. She had to spur her horse into a keawe thicket and emerged dripping blood. When the boys had the bull lassoed and rejoined Mittee, they evinced no more concern over her injuries than they would have over their own. They thought of her as one of them, and no greater respect could have been accorded her.

Edward did not finish his studies at the university. During the Christmas holidays he persuaded his parents to let him remain at home and in January 1925 he married his lovely Maui High School sweetheart, Ruth Lindsay, and took over the managership of Ulupalakua Ranch on May 1, 1925.

The newlyweds moved into the beautiful big house on the ranch, and Mittee and Frank relocated to the small house below.

Edward and Ruth had two children; Gregory, who was to follow in his father's footsteps, and Jane (Mrs. Ralph King). Because of the distance from school and the long winding roads, Greg lived with his grandparents in Spreckelsville for ten years when Kaunoa School was in session. Jane also lived away from her parents during the Kaunoa School term, with her aunt and uncle, Mr. and Mrs. C.H. "Buster" Burnett.

Stable Road: Frank found the commute from Ulupalakua to his work in Puunene entirely too time-consuming, so the Baldwins bought the Serby house on Spreckelsville beach. (Weekends and summers were still spent in Ulupalakua.) Next door to them, separated by a tennis court, was brother Sam Baldwin's house. An exchange of houses was arranged, probably sometime in 1925, and Mittee then began the rebuilding and refurbishing which produced the magnificent Stable Road estate. To this day the property has kept its prestige and is worth an astronomical sum. Mittee missed her calling—she should have been an architect.

Mr. Ah Fook left the Baldwin employ about this time to become cook for the single men at the Paia Club House. Mittee was fortunate to obtain the services of Mr. Kichigo Morimoto and his wife Asa, who remained in the Baldwin household for 30 years. Kichigo was versed in the art of Chinese cuisine. Mittee enjoyed entertaining friends and Frank's many business associates in her home. She hosted the ladies of her husband's staff frequently at teas, and held large and small dinner parties. Her mother had sent her a gift of Medallion china from San Francisco and Mittee acquired more pieces over the years. She could seat and serve 24 guests easily. Frank liked small, intimate groupings, but Mittee enjoyed filling her table to capacity. The cuisine was often but not always Chinese. She served formal dinners on a table covered with damask and sterling and sparkling crystal. Even when Mittee and Frank dined alone the table was elegantly set.

The Prohibition years did not deter Mittee and Frank from providing their guests with alcoholic sustenance. There were always kegs of good aged *okolehao* to tap. "Oke" (whiskey) generally was served in a shot glass accompanied by a water chaser. If the whiskey were exceptionally mellow, it could be served as a liqueur. Frank was never a heavy drinker, but he always said, "Never trust a man who is stingy with his liquor."

Puunene Athletic Club: Shortly after World War I HC&S formed the Puunene Athletic Club and built a beautiful complex of club-

14

house, swimming pool, bowling alley and cottages for the single men joining the plantation staff. Provisions were made for these men to have their meals in the clubhouse dining room. The club became the focal point for supervisory employees of HC&S. Harvest Home and other dances were held there with local groups providing the music. The social circle of Maui was small in those days, so everybody knew everybody else at the Club. Mittee must have been a spectacular dancer, because the family still speaks of her waltzing across the ballroom with Ralph Wilson, another excellent dancer, to the applause of onlookers.

The Club facilities were also available to the general public. The pool was used by Central and East Maui people for swim competitions and the grounds for activities such as ball games and dog shows. There were few other comparable entertainment centers available on the island.

Maui Country Club: As the popularity of the game of golf progressed, it became quite evident that a golf club was needed in Central Maui. In 1925 the 46 members of the Maui Golf Club organized the Maui Country Club at Spreckelsville. A clubhouse was built and two years later a 9-hole golf course was added, designed by architects William McEwan and Alex Bell. Between the Club's organization and the completion of the course Maui Country Club members played on a nine-hole course which then existed at Pauwela.

Frank had played the old Lighthouse course at Pauwela, and liked the game. He established a precedent for a half-day off on Wednesdays for his business executives, so they could golf in the afternoon. The Club drew membership from all of Maui, as it still does.

Frank was only a fair player, but Mittee now took up golf and became a good player. She loved the companionship it afforded, and the exercise. She pulled her own cart although there were caddies available. Until a few years before her death, she kept her clubs in the hope that she would be able to play once again.

Polo came to Maui in 1887 and in 1889 a tournament was held in Makawao. The polo field was just beyond the junction of what is now the Haleakala Highway and Haliimaile Road. It was a large complex complete with caretaker's house, paddock, and stables where the horses were groomed and trained for the game.

Frank was an outstanding polo player. He played with the von Tempsky brothers, Harold Rice, David Fleming, and others, and with his brother-in-law, Arthur Collins. (Arthur was seriously hurt when his newly purchased pony "Rainbow" fell on him during a game. He sustained a severe back injury which apparently was successfully treated by surgery in New York. However, he later died from a bone splinter which lodged in an artery. At that time he was manager of the Pioneer Mill Company. Ethel hated to leave Maui, but ill health necessitated her return to the Mainland. She settled in Santa Barbara with her three children. For the following seven years she and the children returned to spend their summer vacations on Maui with Mittee and the General. The visits lessened as her health declined and she died in 1940.

Many polo games were held on Friday nights at the old Honolulu stadium. Mittee would accompany Frank to Oahu, where he participated in games with Walter MacFarland, Harold Castle, Ii Brown, Walter Dillingham, Harold and Arthur Rice and others. When in Honolulu, they always had an open invitation from their friends Sam and Julia Weller to stay in their home. Sam was a principal in the Consolidated Amusement Company and the Maui Amusement Company, which provided films for movie houses throughout the Territory, and when on Maui he and Julia would be guests of the Frank Baldwins.

Frank's enthusiasm for the game was shared by his three sons who played with their cousins, Oskie Rice and Manduke Baldwin, and with Gordon von Tempsky and other sons of Hawaii's polo-playing families. His grandson Gregory inherited the passion, and played with the best teams in California for many years.

In the 1930's father and sons formed themselves into the famed Baldwin polo team with "The General," as he was now called, as its leader. These were his proudest days—riding with his sons Edward, Asa and Chu, to win championship after championship.

In 1934 Will Rogers visited Hawaii for one week. The following letter appeared in the San Francisco Chronicle on August 1 of that year:

> "KULA MAUI, JULY 31—Editor the Chronicle: Did you ever hear of the Hawaiian Islands. Well if you didn't you have heard of Baldwin's. Flew into an island here that is just chuck full of Baldwins. Frank Baldwin has the biggest sugar plantation and the most up-to-date and best run. A water pumping system that is big as San Francisco. Then they got a big cattle ranch. All riders and ropers and polo players. These visitors that never get away from the Whykiki beach when they come out here miss a lot. This island must have the best politicians. For they got the best roads. Over home a Congressman is never any better than his road. And sometimes worse. Yours, WILL ROGERS."

The closest Mittee came to riding polo ponies was to hitch Frank's two ponies to a carriage in Hamakuapoko. The ride out was without incident, but she lost control on the way home, and carriage and ponies ended up in a *punawai* (reservoir). Mittee was unhurt, but one of the ponies drowned. What Frank said to her is not known, but she never repeated the experiment.

Mittee raised both polo ponies and race horses with the help of Akira Ishikawa, aka "Jockey." Akira was Ulupalakua born and went to work for Edward Baldwin after completing grammar school. He became an excellent horse trainer, a terrific jockey, and Mittee loved him enough to refer to him as her adopted son.

Akira tells of the time he was training a horse at Ulupalakua that jumped a fence, unseated and fell on him. The Ranch foreman at that time was the famous and colorful cowboy Ikua Purdy who was born on the Parker Ranch and hired by Edward at the age of eighteen. Ikua, his son, and Akira's father found Akira lying badly hurt on the ground. Purdy sent for a glass of Hawaiian salt mixed with water which he made the injured man drink before taking him to the hospital. Hawaiian rock salt (Pa-a-kai) is still a staple in Hawaiian homes and is used for medicinal purposes as well as for seasoning. It is a gargle for sore throats, and drunk to relieve pain, even in injuries as serious as fractures.

Mittee bought the finest stock available. From Charlie Howard, who owned Sea Biscuit, she bought three mares; Alice Bird, Battling Jenny and Kapakini. She bred these mares with three studs; Bolinty, Delphinium and Alicane, which she purchased from a marvelous horseman named Neil McCarthy.

At the request of Alfred Wellington Carter, the general manager of the Parker Ranch, Mittee sent Alicane to the island of Hawaii. Mittee always remembered with anger that Alicane returned to Maui in poor shape from overuse. Many of the fine horses which came out of the Parker Ranch were descended from Alicane.

The Baldwins also bought several horses of South American origin, among them a horse named Elastico, from Bing Crosby who had to sell off his stable to pay inheritance taxes after his wife Dixie Lee died. Mittee's careful breeding among these horses produced her most cherished thoroughbred, Aloha Oe.

When the ponies were ready for polo training, they were taken to the field at Haliimaile where an Irishman named Jack Tiernan took over their education. Tiernan was famous for his fiery temper. Many a bench was the victim of his wrath, as was his foot!

Akira always managed to take the ponies down to the field around

Baldwin Polo Team: Asa, Chu, General, Edward

General, Edward, Asa, Chu

Makawao Polo Club: Front: Unidentified, William Huddy, Frank Baldwin, C.B. Copp Jr. 2nd row: Harry F. Baldwin, Judge C.B. Copp, Henry Copp. 3rd row: Von Tempsky, Louie Von Tempsky, next two unidentified

lunchtime, so that the Chinese cook, who was not very pleased about it, would have to prepare food for him too.

There were enough ponies to seat two teams (teams consist of four players). If a pony sustained an injury, there were other mounts available. An injured pony would be taken back to Ulupalakua for treatment by Dr. John Fitzgerald, who was the only veterinarian on Maui for many years.

The General was a soft-spoken man normally, but his language turned the air blue when his pet pony, Freckles, did not come up to expectations.

The fascinating game of polo brought many interesting personalities to Maui. Among them was Major (later to be General) George S. Patten, a hard-driving and terrific rider who played "hell for leather" polo on the U.S. Army team against the Baldwin family team many times. When on Maui he would be the guest of the Edward Baldwins at Ulupalakua Ranch, where, it is said, he once drank a glass of whiskey while standing on his head.

Polo provided much entertainment for the people of Maui. Cars would line up around the Haliimaile field to watch the matches. It was a great family outing. Polo fans were not only interested in the players but in their ponies as well. The following is from the Maui News:

> 1915—Carry the News, Dr. W. D. Baldwin's famous polo pony, and probably the finest polo mount in the world, has been sick for the past 10 days with a severe cold. He is under the care of Dr. Fitzgerald, and is much better at present.

Horseracing: Horseracing was always very popular on Maui until the 1950's when it gradually faded away. Also from the local paper:

> l915—If any doubt existed as to the success of the Maui races and frontier sports events for New Year's, they were swept away. The card as it now stands is a dandy. The horses for the principal events are all now at the Kahului track and are showing fine form.

The annual Maui County Fair races, which took place on the last day of the Fair, always on a Sunday afternoon, were very well attended. Breeders from all the Islands would ship their best thoroughbreds to Maui to compete. There were three-quarter mile races, half-mile races, 1-1/2 mile cowboy races, and half-mile Hawaiian-bred pony races. Mittee's racing silks were green with a red sash, and she kept her attention on those colors during a race. In fact, she kept her attention on every aspect of her horses' care and training—often disagreeing with Akira's views. At these times the General stepped in

Akira Ishikawa with Mittee's Cherrie Bo.
This picture was taken by Geo. C. Wilkins Custom Photography

and smoothed the troubled waters.

The General, President of the Racing Association for eleven years, would be in the middle of the hubbub, and Mittee would be busy about her racing entries. (Racing enthusiasts miss the good old days. The subject of legalized gambling (parimutuel) comes up in the Hawaiian legislature often, but nothing ever comes of it. The consensus seems to be that people have better ways to spend their money than to lose it at horseraces.)

The first Maui County Fair was held in Wailuku in 1916. The only ride it offered was on the back of Daisy, the elephant from the Honolulu Zoo, also known as "The Virgin of Waikiki." Daisy could carry only three or four children at one time. A long line of patient children waited for their turn.

Mittee was most definitely instrumental in bringing Akira downcountry to be her right-hand man and to work for the Plantation. The stable and paddocks were right below the alfalfa barn at the entrance to Stable Road. He was in charge of the care of the horses used by the plantation *lunas* (bosses) and of the mules for the spray gangs.

Also from Ulupalakua came a girl named Fumiko. Upon her graduation from the eighth grade at the age of 14 she was employed by the Baldwins, and it was here on Stable Road that she met her future husband. Masaru Fukushima first worked next door for Harold Rice and later became Caddy Master at the Maui Country Club for six or seven years. When Matsui, the Baldwin's first chauffeur, returned to Japan, Masaru took his place and became driver and handyman for Mittee and the General. He was on call 24 hours a day, more or less. The Fukushimas became very close members of the Baldwin family.

The General was a dedicated plantation man. Filling his father's shoes was not easy. To manage one of the largest cane-sugar producing plantations in the world, he needed the best help he could find. He reported to his office in Puunene daily. He applied his enormous prestige to serving the sugar industry and his beloved Hawaii. Frank loved people and his charities were many. Not least among his accomplishments was the engineering of a program for the improvement of plantation employee's living conditions.

Housing, medical facilities, day nurseries, parks, playgrounds and the dairy became the finest of their kind in Hawaii. HC&S employees were among the first such workers to have electricity in their homes. Filtered domestic water, sewer systems, churches, theaters, clubhouses and swimming pools were added over the years. It was his interest which motivated the development of a model town for employees in Kahului, aptly dubbed "Dream City."

Frank had incredibly many responsibilities. He was the manager and president of HC&S Co; president of the Kahului Railroad Company, Baldwin Packers, Ltd. and Ulupalakua Ranch. He became a director of Alexander & Baldwin in 1918, and its president from 1947 until 1960. He was vice-president of the East Maui Irrigation Company, Ltd., director of the Hawaiian Trust Company, and managing director of Henry P. Baldwin, Ltd. (This was a holding company established by his father consolidating his A&B interests for the benefit of his heirs.) He played a leading role in the work of the Maui Planters' Association and the Hawaiian Sugar Planters' Association.

In the civic and social arenas, he was president of the Maui County Fair and Racing Association and president of the Maui Chamber of Commerce. He was a member of the Hawaii Polo and Racing Association, the Oahu Country Club; the Pacific Club, University Club, Commercial Club of Honolulu, Maui Country Club and the Rotary Club of Maui.

His successful handling of the bewildering array of work responsibilities among the affiliated companies was due in part to his keen understanding of human nature. He was able to choose the right person for the right job and so could confidently delegate authority. His subtle sense of humor and the sparkle in his eye also helped him to survive the good and bad years of boom and depression, war and peace, in a Hawaii which changed in his time from kingdom to territory to state.

Mittee spent much of her time serving the Maui Community. She was the first Commissioner of the Maui Council of Girl Scouts; a position which she held for thirteen years. Serving on the council with her were her sister-in-law, Charlotte Rice, and her sister Ethel Collins. During this period the girl scouts organized a drum and bugle corps. This group for several years provided the only music that the County of Maui could muster for its Memorial Day parades. Irma Gerner Burns, who later became Mittee's companion for almost twenty years, was a member of this corps.

The plantation took an active interest in the Girl Scouts. The manager of the East Maui Irrigation Company donated land to it for a campsite in Kailua, and the plantations provided trucks to transport the girls. It was a lovely, narrow strip of land extending upward from the main highway; bordered in by towering green cliffs above, a tangled forest of kukui and ferns on one side, and a gulch on the other. A series of waterfalls splashed down 150 feet of rocky paths to feed a natural pool. The memory of Camp Pokuelani will be cherished as long as there is a girl scout or a brownie alive who spent a summer vacation there. A severe earthquake in 1938 damaged the site so badly that it had to be abandoned.

Makawao Union Church Activities: Mittee was also active in the Ladies' Aid Society of the Makawao Union Church, which held a bazaar every November. The women worked all year long preparing for the event and their talents in baking and crafts earned many dollars for many good causes. Mittee supplied food for the lunches until so many women were attending that catering was needed; but Mittee continued to pick up the tab. She loved the bazaars, for the treasures she could buy there and for meeting the many Maui people who supported the church; in particular the old-time plantation wives.

Although the General was a Trustee of the Makawao Union Church, he was not a member. He attended service with Mittee every Sunday, sitting always in the same pew, which was strategically situated for him to be able to count heads. The only time he missed service was when it conflicted with Ulupalakua's annual picnic. Reverend Ross Cleeland remembers shaking hands with the General after church every week. The reverend would always ask him how things were, and he would invariably reply either: "Hot as hell" or "Cold as hell" attempting (and failing) teasingly to shock the minister.

Mittee was also interested in other religious beliefs. She was an ardent pupil of Christian Science, Transcendental Meditation, and (with her sister-in-law Katherine Baldwin) the Baha'i Spiritual Assembly. Her long-time spiritual advisors were Dr. Joel Goldsmith and Dr. Joseph Murphy.

Family Pets: And Mittee's love of dogs must be mentioned, since raising them to be shown was another activity which occupied her time. Fumiko can remember her having at one time as many as eight dogs—pointers, setters, afghan hounds, and a Chinese black chow named Wee Sing, which the General adored. Wee Sing was especially devoted to him at mealtime. Frank sincerely denied slipping tidbits to him, but fooled nobody.

Later the Baldwins acquired two pomeranians, and still later Mittee's beloved corgies, John, Grey and Marty. (Two monkeys were also part of the Stable Road menage, named Harry and Ethel after the Harry A. Baldwins.)

Maui had a very active kennel club which annually held a dog show and obedience trials on the Puunene Clubhouse grounds. Frank Sato, an expert handler of dogs from Honolulu, would come to Maui to show her entries. Mittee's dogs were also entered into Oahu competitions. She always accompanied them there, and personally turned them over to Sato. Another Honolulu friend, Arthur Zane, was a dog fancier and helped Mittee with her hobby. It was he who helped her acquire the corgies, which were from Australia.

Family Update: Asa Baldwin completed his education at Yale University in 1929 and returned to Maui. He was first employed by Maui Agricultural Company in Paia as irrigation overseer, then as relief luna, and later as division overseer in Keahua. He was appointed assistant manager in 1938 and remained in that capacity until the retirement of his uncle Harry A. Baldwin in 1946 when he succeeded him as manager. He married Virginia Frothingham Castle of Oahu on August 18, 1933. They had two sons, Michael and John.

Son Chu (Lawrence) graduated from Yale in 1933. Upon his return to Maui he joined Hawaiian Commercial & Sugar Company as water luna, then relief luna, after which he became Welfare Director and subsequently Personnel Director. He was an especially charming man, universally liked, and in 1938 was elected to the Maui County Board of Supervisors. He married Margaret May McGrew on September 2, 1935. They had two daughters, Mariette (Mrs. Harry B. Hollins) and Laurien (Mrs. John Callender).

Day To Day: The General's day began very early at his office in Puunene. After he scanned his daily appointment schedule, he called the McGerrow Stable, where a horn alerted the stableman to deliver his horse to the Main Office. As his father had done before him, he then rode through the fields before returning to his office for appointments with various managers of the affiliated companies, or staff meetings, or visits with people who would drop in to ask for a particular favor. (On one occasion he called his secretary and instructed her to bring him fifty dollars, which he gave to the man in his office. When the man had left with the money, he called her again to ask: "Do you know who that man was?")

He wrote daily to the manager of A&B to keep the agency informed of all plantation activities. (All Maui mail was "boat mail" then, and most letters left the Island on Monday and Thursday.) The post office occupied the major portion of the Main Office's Makai (seaward) wing, which was most convenient. When the present Puunene post office was built across the street, the postmaster personally delivered Frank's mail.

Generally in the afternoon he would meet with D.T. Fleming from Honolua, who would update him on Baldwin Packers' affairs. Edward would call weekly to report on Ulupalakua Ranch business. He met often with William Walsh (affectionately called "the Mayor of Kahului") to discuss Railroad business.

(In 1935 the Kahului Railroad Company replaced its passenger trains with busses for the convenience of Central Maui and Upcountry people. It was never much used and the operation was suspended. The Railroad was also the agent for Inter-Island Airways and for the steamship company. Steamer and plane reservations were obtainable at the Railroad's Main Office in Kahului — travel agencies were yet to come to Maui.)

Since the General, like all Plantation personnel, arose so early, his office day was over at four o'clock. He routinely went home and had a bit of a nap before joining Mittee for cocktails before dinner and an occasional walk in the garden.

Every Saturday afternoon the Baldwins took in the movie at the old Kahului Theater on the corner of Puunene and Kaahumanu Avenues that replaced the Kahului Lyceum Theater which burned down in 1917. They had permanently reserved seats. The peculiarity of this cinema was that the show never began until William Walsh and his wife Mabel arrived.

As can be seen, most of Frank's time was scheduled. If he found himself with a free afternoon he would drive to Kihei, never failing to offer a ride to anyone who was walking. One of his favorite stories concerned picking up an old man on the old beach road in Kihei. When they arrived at his destination, the old man said, "Thank you Mr. Baldwin." Frank said, "Don't mention it." The old man replied, "I no tell nobody."

The General's personal contributions to the churches of Maui, and those he authorized from the Plantation, were considerable. He also enjoyed visits from the clergy. Reverend Abraham Akaka (then pastor of the Kahului Union Church) called often before transferring to the Kawaiahao Church in Honolulu. Father Bax of the Puunene Catholic Church was a good friend of many years standing. When the need arose for a Catholic church in Kahului, the General offered him a beach front property near Kahului Harbor, but the Father preferred a site further inland; safe from the danger of tidal waves. In

1931 he was given an appropriate property, and Christ the King Church was built in 1932. When Father Bax decided to return to his homeland, Frank paid for the trip. (The Father died in his beloved Holland in 1956.)

A number of times the General helped employees who were in financial binds. One such instance concerned a young man named Robert H. Hughes. Frank supplied monetary assistance for his education, and he did the General proud. He rose steadily in the industry, ultimately attaining the presidency of the Hawaii Sugar Planters' Association. Frank also helped with the education of some young men who were unconnected with the plantation.

The Baldwins traveled frequently; to Honolulu, the Mainland and all parts of the world. (In college, Frank and his brother Arthur toured Switzerland. While in the Alps, they had a little argument [as brothers do] about which of them should carry the travelers' checks. After some snatching back and forth, the checks fell into a crevasse, and that settled the argument.)

World War II: Akira was one of the first Maui men of the 100th Infantry Battalion to be sent to the front in Europe. His Company encountered the enemy in a forest and the men were ordered to hit the turf, but a ricocheting bullet struck Akira in an embarrassing place. He returned to Maui in 1945 and Mittee put him to work immediately. He still could not sit a horse comfortably and wanted to ride standing up, but Mittee would not hear of it, so a soft sheepskin was rigged to the saddle for him.

The war brought many people to Maui and into the Baldwins' lives, some of whom became lifelong friends. The General negotiated the leasing of land to the government for the Puunene and the Kahului Naval Air Stations. Mittee became a Red Cross Grey Lady. Through her powerful connections, she was in large part responsible for making Camp Maui in Kokomo a delightful place for the men who came there for Rest and Recreation.

Then Mittee added another hobby to her already full life; painting. Her instructor was Mr. Fujimoto (then a teacher at Baldwin High School), who held classes for many interested Maui women. He swears she had talent, but in the author's view she was no Grandma Moses. However, art was a relaxing pursuit. She painted in her little studio, away from the main house, on Stable Road.

In the Wake of the War: The happiness that the war was over and won was of short duration for the Baldwin family. In 1946, Chu collapsed and died of a heart attack after a strenuous game of squash on his home court. Chu, as Frank's assistant manager, was being groomed to succeed his father. Hearts were heavy. It was especially difficult for Frank at his office because of the daily contact with his son. The complexities of management helped ease his sorrow somewhat, and life had to go on.

In Chu's memory, his parents and the Puunene and East Maui Community Associations jointly sponsored college scholarships for promising children of employees and pensioners of HC&S. After Frank's death, Mittee continued her contributions, and took pleasure in the gratitude expressed by many recipients.

Tsunami: Then in 1946 came a devastating tidal wave. The author is indebted to Fumiko Fukushima for the information on its impact on Stable Road.

It was early in the morning on April Fools' Day. In the Fukushima household, Fumiko was preparing breakfast and getting her children ready to send off to school. Masaru was already out working. Fumiko's father, who was living with the family, glanced outside and saw the first wave rolling in, twisting and turning like serpents. It was terrifying! Immediately the water was upon them. Large rocks were floating as if they were light as sponges, and fish were swimming all over the yard. The cottages of their neighbors, the Kamemotos and the Morimotos, situated on low ground, were half covered with water. Fortunately the Fukushima house was on higher ground, and although the water rose about five feet, the family was able to remain in the house. Even so, their front steps were swept away.

Masaru was washing the General's work car in the four-car garage. The cars began floating around like toys. Masaru made for the Baldwin house and found the General in front watching the tidal wave. Frank told him that the tidal wave of 1923 had not been too bad; only a foot or so high, and that he thought there was no cause for worry. When Masaru saw the second wave, he realized this was no small *tsunami*. He pushed the General into the living room of the house, and then ran through the house and out the kitchen door, to get home. It was impossible. The wave had hit and if there had been no coconut fronds to hang on to, he would have been swept away. He made his way back into the house and found the General, who had been washed through a glass wall into the small patio. Miraculously, the only injury Frank suffered was a gashed forehead. Mittee was in her little cottage in a wing adjacent to the main house at the time and that part of the house was undamaged.

The dogs were kenneled between the kitchen and Masaru's cottage, on low ground. When Fumiko could get to them, the area was a pond, with the dogs swimming around in it. The wave had knocked down the monkeys' cage, and Ethel and Harry had done what came naturally and climbed a tree. (They could not be coaxed down. They made themselves at home on Masaru's roof, and occasionally, if the opportunity arose, came down to pull his hair. Mittee finally got a man from Puunene to retrieve them. She gave him the monkeys but went to visit them from time to time.) Everyone was picked up and taken to the triangle on Hana Highway, just above the alfalfa barn, and returned home only when it was deemed safe.

The second wave had done the most damage. Much of the furniture in the Baldwin house was ruined by mud and debris. Many of the furnishings were lodged in the sand and recovered later. Much work had to be done on the house before it could be occupied again.

Gashed forehead notwithstanding, the General was concerned about the beach residents in the Spreckelsville and Paia areas and reported to his office. He arranged for plantation personnel to assist tidal wave victims and to open private company roads for general use. The water and debris damage to the Hana Highway made it necessary for traffic through the Paia area to drive the higher plantation roads. Then he went to the hospital to have his injury attended to.

The Kamemoto, Morimoto and Fukushima families cleaned up their residences and were able to occupy them. Mittee and the General had to move into the Cotton House at the Puunene Naval Air Station. (It had been the commander's house during the war.) Mittee was quite accustomed to adjusting to moves, and went on with business as usual until her home was repaired.

It was soon evident that the tidal wave's impact had injured the General more than had been thought. He was hospitalized with thrombosis in his left leg. (Dr. William Patterson, who treated him, urgently needed a blood-thinning agent which was only obtainable from the hospital in Lahaina—usually a 45 minute drive from Wailuku. He gave Masaru 30 minutes to return with the medicine. Masaru was familiar with the road, having driven many Baldwin guests to Mala Wharf to catch their boats to Honolulu. Still, it must have taken extraordinary skill, determination, and concern for the General to make the round trip in that short time.) The General was never his old self after this illness, although he worked just as conscientiously as ever.

Late in 1947 he informed J. Platt Cooke, manager of Alexander & Baldwin, that he believed a merger of HC&S and Maui Agricultural Company would benefit both companies. The Hawaiian sugar industry had evolved from the gradual merging of many small plantations into major plantations. The merger was approved, and on April 1, 1948, the General resigned as manager of HC&S, and his son Asa succeeded to the position. Frank retained the presidency, as well as his positions in the affiliated companies. His new office was across from the Bougainvillea-covered building—the old vault housing the plantation archives.

Triggered by the merger, the following article appeared in the April 5th, l948 issue of Time Magazine which deserves quoting in its entirety:

SUGAR
King of the Canebrakes

Acre for acre, the red lava soil of Hawaii is the richest sugar land in the world. Two of Hawaii's biggest sugar plantations on the island of Maui, are Hawaiian Commercial & Sugar Co., Ltd. and Maui Agricultural Co., Ltd. Last week 70-year old Frank Fowler Baldwin, ruling patriarch of Hawaii's potent Alexander & Baldwin, Ltd., combined the two companies in a $25 million merger. As a result, the new company, Hawaiian Commercial & Sugar Co., Ltd., with 25,454 acres of cane land and a yearly output of 135,000 tons of sugar, becomes the largest plantation on the islands.

Over the Gulch. The ancient Hawaiians had long grown sugar cane on the islands, but it was New England missionaries like Baldwin's grandfather Dwight (he came in 1831) who brought Yankee traders to commercialize it. It was Dwight's son, bushy-bearded, one-armed Henry Baldwin (he lost the other arm in a cane-mangler) who built the Baldwin dynasty. He went partners with Sam Alexander, son of another missionary. At a cost of $80,000 and harrowing effort, Henry built the 17-mile-long Hamakua Ditch to bring irrigation in the cane fields. With son Frank, he once swam a flooded gulch in order to get to church. Through such God-fearing boldness, coupled with Yankee-trader shrewdness, the business prospered, became one of the "Big Five"* which reach across the biggest part of Hawaii's economy.

Today the Alexander & Baldwin interests extend into shipping, hotels, communications, oil, banking, one-tenth of all Hawaiian pineapple, one-eight of the island sugar. Since Henry Baldwin's death in 1911, the empire has been ruled by stocky Frank Baldwin (the Alexanders are no longer active in the management). Frank is training his own son, Asa, 40, to carry on. Last week, Asa moved into the new company as his father's second in command.

Over the Hurdle? Both the merged companies, though separately owned, were already controlled by the complex building company pyramid of the Alexander and Baldwin families. In putting both companies into one corporate pocket, Frank Baldwin had several cogent reasons.

Hawaiian sugar plantations are the world's most productive, but their costs have long been among the world's highest, too. They were increased by the organizing inroads of the C.I.O.'s Harry Bridges. Average pay for the industry is $8.10 a day. In a boom year like 1947, when Hawaiian Commercial & Sugar netted $2,200,000, Maui Agricultural $800,000, that was not an insuperable handicap. But recently world sugar has shown signs of returning to its "normal" condition of overproduction. The Hawaiian price has fallen from its wartime high of $126.40 per ton to $108, seems likely to tumble more. With this prospect, Hawaii's planters must somehow cut their costs. Increased mechanization has helped. Last week's merger, said Baldwin, would 1) wipe out duplicate bookkeeping and other management functions, 2) make for a more efficient distribution of the 400 million gallons of water which another Baldwin-controlled company annually sends through the irrigation system started by old Henry's Hamakua Ditch.

The others: American Factors, Ltd., Castle & Cooke, Ltd., C. Brewer & Co., Ltd., Theo H. Davies & Co., Ltd.

The General was as busy as ever. It should be noted that he was an enthusiastic Rotarian who enjoyed his Wednesday luncheon meetings. The president of the club would phone Frank's secretary to remind him to bring money to pay the fines he incurred for his humorous infractions. He was delighted to pay for what he regarded as a special honor.

Golden Anniversaries: The Baldwins' 50th wedding anniversary on April 27, 1950, was marked by a celebration at the Paholei home of Frank Churchill. Friends came from all the islands. It is not remembered how many guests attended, but that it was a spectacular party is well remembered.

Then, in 1951, the General and Asa, co-hosting with their plantation family, held an HC&S Jubilee Celebration and invited all of Maui to attend. HC&S had much to celebrate; the golden anniversary of the Puunene mill and the 100th anniversary of the first sugar mill in the area (Spreckelsville). The Island had never seen such a party. Ten thousand people enjoyed tours of the mill and consumed thousands of hot dogs and bottles of soda pop. The transportation committee had its work cut out for it, because nobody wanted to go home. The busses supplied by the plantation were running half an hour to an hour late, but nobody really minded.

The Stable Road home had weathered several small tidal waves since the big one in 1946 and the Baldwins had stayed on. However, a larger one in 1952, although it did no significant damage was one too many for Frank and Mittee. Asa had acquired his grandparents' Maluhia home in 1947, and the Frank Churchills, victims of the '46 wave, had occupied his Spreckelsville home until their Paholei home was completed. This home, which had been a wedding gift to Asa from his mother and father was comparatively safe from *tsunamis,* close to work and to the centers of activity. It was an ideal move for Mittee and Frank and became their last residence.

HC&S Diamond Jubilee: Probably the biggest private party ever held on Maui marked HC&S's 75th year on April 3, 1957. A huge cake graced the Main Office patio in Puunene, decorated with an iced plastic model of the Puunene Mill. According to Nashiwa's Bakery, that cake was the largest ever baked on Maui. Batter, icing, layer separators and the base made it weigh 1,400 pounds. (The recipe for it read like a wholesale grocery order: 281 lbs granulated sugar; 57 lbs creamery butter; 53 lbs vegetable shortening; 175 lbs cake flour; 1,260 whole eggs plus 1,320 egg whites; 9 lbs of baking soda, and 80 lbs of powdered sugar for the icing. This provided about 1,500 slices. Another 57 square cakes were needed to provide the 5,148 slices served. These were washed down by 5,712 bottles of soda pop.)

All supervisors and off-duty personnel were invited to attend the cake-cutting by President Frank Baldwin that morning, and supervisors on all three shifts conveyed cake and soda to their crews.

About this time another honor was bestowed on the General; "The award of Mamalahoe Kanawai (The Law of the Splintered Paddle)." This was one of Kamehameha's most famous decrees. The story goes that during a raid in Puna, Kamehameha caught his foot in a crevice in the lava when he was chasing an innocent fisherman. The fisherman turned about, struck Kamehameha on the head with a paddle and escaped. Later, Kamehameha's men caught the fisherman, and Kamehameha admitted he had attacked an innocent person, gifted the fisherman with land, and then decreed: "Let the aged, men and women, and little children lie down in safety in the road. Let no one molest them. The penalty is death." Bestowing this honor on Frank Baldwin acknowledged his life-long esteem for the people of his island and Hawaii.

Not to neglect Mittee; it was the custom each year, when the mills began the grinding season, that the manager's wife pull the switch which started the wheels rolling. In 1952 the two HC&S mills began grinding at exactly the same time. Mittee, as wife of the HC&S president, was asked to pull the switch at Puunene, while Tooty (Asa's wife's nickname), pulled its counterpart in Paia.

(Apropos of the demise of this custom, this article appeared in the June, 1961, issue of the publication, HC&S Breeze:

HC&S Diamond Jubilee, Mittee and the General. HC&S Co. Breeze Photo.

Mittee and Pomeranians

The General

THEY LAUGH ABOUT IT — NOW

Have you wondered why HC&S dropped the rites that once started the grinding season? Although attempts were made to revive the custom, the last really full-scale mill opening at Puunene was on January 14, 1952. Since that embarrassing day, Mill Department Head Bob Hughes has preferred to start the season gradually and, if possible, in private.

Present in 1952 was a crowd of notables—other plantation managers, County officials, and the press. After the usual speeches, Mr. Hughes personally conducted Mrs. Frank Baldwin, wife of the company's president, to the starting button. Flash bulbs exploded. Cameras clicked. Mrs. Baldwin smiled radiantly and pressed the button firmly.

The mill whistle roared. Everyone waited expectantly. Nothing happened.

Mrs. Baldwin pressed the button again. Still nothing happened.

There were shouts above and below. Men rushed up and down the catwalks. Ten minutes passed. Finally a few cane stalks came through the shredder knives. Then everything stopped dead.

Long after the last amused guest departed, Mr. Hughes discovered that someone forgot to tell the mill engine tender about the ceremony. The tender was supposed to open up the main steam valve when the whistle blew. Unfortunately, he wasn't anywhere around when he was needed.

As pleasant as it is to relate stories of humor and honors, tragedy intrudes itself with regularity. In 1956, Edward Baldwin became ill and died. Boy von Tempsky took over the management of the ranch until Gregory completed his college education and returned home.

The merger of the two plantations occasioned many changes. The Paia Hospital, built in 1909, became an orphanage, and the Puunene Hospital assumed the medical needs of employees. A dispensary adjacent to the Paia Mill handled emergencies for the neighborhood. For those unable to get to Puunene Hospital, village nurses were on continual call to provide care or, if needed, transportation to the hospital. There were "Duty Doctors" on call. (Physicians' home phone numbers were not unlisted in those days.) The doctors would make house calls if deemed necessary, or would arrange for the patient to be admitted to the hospital; first to Puunene Hospital, then after it was closed, to Maui Memorial. Also, the Maui Clinic was formed and maintained by the plantation.

The Paia store, a Maui institution for so many years, moved to Kahului, where the majority of employees now lived. Shopping in a supermarket and a merchandising mart was far different from having groceries and goods delivered by plantation stores. The days of "bango" charges and deductions in pay envelopes from the Main Office for store purchases were over. In the October 9, issue of the

HC&S Breeze, the following appeared:

A&B Stores Open All Day Wednesday

Two new customer service policies, keeping all stores open Wednesday afternoons, and offering wholesale customers low cash and carry prices, were announced by A&B Commercial Company. All stores were open for business all day Wednesday for the first time October 6. In the past A&B Paia, Puunene, and Kihei closed at noon Wednesday.

In 1957, Mittee had an accident in which she broke two ribs. She read that (then) Senator Richard Nixon had slipped on the ice and also had broken ribs. Misery loving company, she wrote him a letter of sympathy and received an immediate answer. "Imagine," she told people, "he may be our next President." Later she would not believe, until unbelief was no longer possible, that he was involved in the Watergate scandal.

The General began slowing down about this time. Mittee would spend her afternoons driving him to Kihei and Lahaina and to the other places he had routinely gone alone. He depended more on her judgment, and his fondness for her deepened. He had a pet name for her which no one else dared use. At one time she had been heavy, and only after she lost the weight did he call her, "Fatty."

Christmas of 1959 was as festive as ever. The General was still working, and HC&S put up a Christmas tree on the Puunene Athletic Club grounds, fronting the HC&S Main Office. It was the tallest tree the company had ever erected. It towered 50 feet into the sky. Its spectacular multi-colored lights and large ornaments drew admirers from all over Maui.

The General's health was slipping away. Shortly after the holidays, on Tuesday, January 26 of 1960, he suffered a fall at home which inflicted a serious neck injury. At first it seemed as if he were recovering, but a paralysis set in which became progressive. Dr. Ralph B. Cloward, a Honolulu neurosurgeon, was summoned to Maui Memorial Hospital to perform emergency surgery on his neck in an attempt to save his life. Again he seemed to rally, but on Saturday morning, February 6, he died.

Beautiful Makawao Union Church, where the General occupied a favorite rear pew every Sunday, was the scene of one of two funeral services. There the Reverend Ross Cleeland led a simple ceremony. The church was jammed with mourning relatives, friends, and employees. Later a service for members of Mr. Baldwin's family was held at Makawao Cemetery where his ashes were interred.

Frank's benign influence spanned a long period of history. From horse-and-buggy days to the era of nuclear fission and orbiting satellites. Today's Hawaii—and tomorrow's, was shaped by this marvelous man and his concern for its industry and its people. His passing left an empty place in the hearts of all who knew him.

After Frank's Death: Not too long after the General died, Asa relinquished his managership of HC&S, still retaining the presidency, to be able to devote more time to personal and family concerns. He had achieved his desired goal. The development of Central Maui was a reality. "Dream City" was built. He had followed his father's and grandfather's road, serving his industry and his Hawaii.

Asa had hopes that his sons would wish to continue in the family tradition. His older son, Michael, a quiet, conscientious and conservative young man, following his graduation from Harvard was being groomed to assume family leadership. After 12 years of employment at HC&S, he decided he was not suited for plantation life and resigned to start his private Management Consulting business. Later he left Maui to establish himself on the Mainland.

Kolohe (rascal) "Johnny," the second son, who inherited the temperament of his Uncle Chu and the feistiness of his grandmother Mittee, amazingly lived to grow to maturity. After brief employment with the Kahului Railroad Company he left to form his own transportation company and became a very successful entrepreneur.

Asa was devoted to his mother. He and Tooty (Virginia) persuaded her to accompany them on a trip to the Orient. From Tokyo, they traveled to Hiroshima to visit with Yuki Kamemoto, who held a permanent place in the hearts of the Baldwin family. Upon their return to Tokyo, Mittee lost her footing on the steps leading to their hotel, and again suffered fractured ribs. Yuki came immediately to tend her, and it was a blessing for the two women to be able to have each other's companionship once again. Accident notwithstanding, Mittee thoroughly enjoyed her trip.

After the Orient trip, Asa asked his secretary, Irma Burns, if she would look in on his mother once a week to field any problems she might have. Since Irma's previous acquaintance with Mittee had been only through her association with the General, she was delighted to find the relationship maturing into true friendship. Irma was Maui born, and had many interests in common with Mittee, who was so young in outlook that the two women thought of each other as contemporaries. Irma now found herself, with cook Lillian Cassel, housekeeper Mildred Watanabe and Masaru, Mittee's chauffeur and constant friend, a member of the family.

Mittee and Irma

In July of 1960 Mittee was traveling again. She met Ethel Baldwin and her nurse Mickey (Eileen MacHenry), and Mrs. James Dole (widow of Lanai's Jim Dole) in New York. The women took a cruise aboard the "Coronia" to Iceland and Scandinavia, among other European ports, and England. Ethel was a teetotaler.

Mittee and Mickey were not, and they had quite a good time together. In England Mittee enjoyed the company of her long-time spiritual advisor, Dr. Joel Goldsmith. All in all, there was a bit too much partying for Mittee at her age, and she did not feel wonderful during the voyage back, but Mickey doctored her fairly well, and she was recovered by the time they reached New York. (Mittee related that Mrs. Dole had always been the first to leave the ship in port, and the first to return to it.)

After the enjoyment of the trip, Mittee was unprepared to hear that her family would have to part with Ulupalakua. When the F.F. Baldwin estate was settled, the family found it would have to be sold to pay inheritance taxes. Mittee was devastated. This meant that the ranch, which had been her life, was gone, and that her grandson Greg would have to establish himself elsewhere.

Mittee now seemed to need to travel more. She took many trips to California. She visited her financial advisor and trusted friend, Wellington Henderson of the Boston-Henderson Company in San Francisco, and Greg, who had relocated in Burlingame, and many other friends in the area. She would visit niece Mary Dawson (Ethel's daughter), in Los Angeles. She made frequent trips to Honolulu, to visit with another niece, Patricia Metcalf, and a nephew, Walter Collins. Her housekeeper, Mildred, generally accompanied her on these trips, and kept Mittee looking like the grand old lady she was.

Ethel's three children were very devoted and each played a very important part in Mittie's well-being. Walter Collins, prominent planner of many business and resort developments in Hawaii, was of great comfort and assistance; Myra, with her many social endeavors in and around Los Angeles kept her apprised of her many acquaintances in that area; Patricia, the avid equestrian, kept her knowledgeable of the world she so dearly loved.

In 1966, Asa became ill and died. Now in her late eighties, Mittee had lost every last one of her immediate family. Her grief was never displayed, nor would she permit the grief of others to be displayed in her presence. What sorrow she felt inwardly was her own, and to be kept to herself. She was fortunate, however, in that her sons had left her a legacy of six grandchildren and twenty great-grandchildren.

Mittee was gifted with the ability to enjoy living. She had few idle moments, what with visits from old war-time acquaintances and her love of partying. She rarely talked about herself, and one of her most valuable assets was the ability to be an interested listener. For the convenience of her many houseguests she purchased a Chevrolet which she named "Annie"—a humorous contraction for "An Emergency."

She settled into a routine of charitable activities, socializing and shopping. She did her own marketing at Ah Fook's, visiting there with the wife of her former cook, discussing the superiority of one cabbage head over another with other shoppers. People were naturally drawn to her.

Her charities on Maui were still many, believing as she did that they should "stay to home." There were individual people whom she supported financially, and she was a generous gift giver both to people and to causes. One of her causes was to assist Laurance Rockefeller and the Nature Conservancy to acquire the Seven Sacred Pools in Kipahulu. In this connection, she was one of his honored guests at a celebration at his Mauna Kea Hotel on the island of Hawaii.

Her interest in the Maui Humane Society never waned, and she was cited by the American Humane Society for 25 years of outstanding service. In 1977 she chaired a special fund drive for the organization.

Her love of racing survived her active participation in the sport. She was glued to the radio every year on the day of the Triple Crown races. Winning or losing $2.00 bets added all the spice she needed to feel intensely involved. The immortal "Secretariat" was her all-time dream horse.

Of her many old friends, two were especially dear to her—Judge Edna Jenkins and Nellie Jean Hegler. They got together frequently, usually for cocktails and *pupus,* at each other's homes. Their get-togethers were not like church socials; there was nothing prim or prissy about these elderly matrons.

Of course family visited often, especially Tooty, Asa's widow, who remained very devoted. Mittee loved to don her "best" dress and have Masaru drive her to Tooty's to a party. Masaru was in charge of logistics then. He was very friendly with Tooty's employees and would pitch in and help. When it came time to leave he also had enjoyed the party.

Irma often drove Mittee to Lahaina; to lunch at the Royal Lahaina

Hotel (they took turns picking up the tab), then to clothes shop at Carol and Mary's and hit any other shop that struck their fancy on the way home.

There has been no occasion yet to mention that Mittee was also a devotee of fine music. She gave generously to the Maui Philharmonic Society and attended all its concerts. She was one of a group of women who participated in a "Morning Music" day. Each hostess in turn would prepare a program of classical music of about four hours' duration, broken by an intermission during which cakes and coffee would be served.

Her Sundays were full of activity. She continued to attend service at Makawao Union Church, in the company of her cook, Lillian Cassel, who was also of the congregation. After church, she would join a close group of friends for a long lunch at the Maui Country Club.

Although she still held a few catered evening cocktail parties and suppers, after the General died, Mittee preferred holding lunch parties. Her prejudicial view of birthday celebrations finally wore out when she reached 98, proving false the long-held idea that she did not know her birth date or age. She had a party, prepared by her home staff, which was so satisfying to her that it had to be repeated when she reached 99. Her father would never have approved.

Mittee's general health was good, except for the onset of glaucoma. The dimming of her sight frightened her, as her mother had been left totally blinded after eye surgery. Driving was now out of the question, and that loss of independence caused her the most concern. She accommodated to the use of a magnifying lens. The signature lines of her checks were underlined heavily in black, so she could see to endorse them with the help of the glass. Her signature was strong, steady and legible. The newspaper was read to her, she listened to the news on radio and TV, and the Library of the Blind sent her Talking Books. A good friend read her the book "The Godfather," a top-seller in her time, which was a real treat.

While lunching with friends at the Maui Lu Hotel in Kihei, something was said to irritate Mittee, and she stormed out of the hotel in high dudgeon—too fast for her years, unfortunately. She fell on the steps and fractured her hip. This was her first serious illness. Like many robust people, she was not very tolerant of anyone's illness, and most people who were sick knew better than to talk to Mittee about it. Of course she hated being in the hospital, and took it out on everybody.

Her good friends braved her temper and brought her cocktails and pupus every day to raise her spirits. Her mail was delivered to her daily. Her home was being well-run by her help, who may have even enjoyed this time as somewhat of a vacation.

When she returned home, Ed Underwood, her doctor and friend, insisted that she have round-the-clock nurses. There were now just too many women in the house, getting in each others' way. Everyone was relieved when the day came that Mittee graduated to a cane, and the house returned to its normal complement of occupants. Lillian and Mildred were capable of handling any night care she might need and it wasn't long before she was able to take long walks in the garden again.

Masaru had officially retired in November of 1974, after 46 years of service with HC&S. He had served as chauffeur to the Baldwins since 1928. Even after retirement he continued to drive his friend Mittee. But now he underwent major surgery, and other companions had to be found for her.

The highlight of Mittie's 99th year was an invitation from Robert "Bobby" Pfeiffer, long-time friend and President of Alexander & Baldwin, extending the honor of official greeter at the ceremony of the S.S. Maui's voyage into Kahului Harbor to show her flag. This amazing woman of so many years charmed the entire audience.

The time inevitably came when she could no longer socialize away from home. She continued to exercise by walking several times around the circle in her front yard. Friends and family visited her and she was content.

About a week before Christmas of 1978, she entered the hospital, and on December 27, a month before her 100th birthday, Mittee died. Her ashes were buried beside her husband's in Makawao.

She had emerged from strong, intelligent and energetic stock. She loved her life, and shared her humor and substance. She enjoyed the better, and stoically endured the bitter, and, with her husband, helped build the Maui and Hawaii of today.

Mittee at her 99th birthday

Mildred and Lillian

Right: Masaru and Mittee

YESTERDAYS

The charm and growth of Maui portrayed in the following articles are very much a segment of the Frank Baldwin family. Under the fine editorship of Harrison Foss, they were published in the HC&S Breeze in the l950's and merit reproduction. The Reign of The Sugar King came from the A&B Ampersand; the Witness to a Century of Service was authored by Rev. Ross B. Cleeland who also contributed many of his memories of Mittee and the General. Mahalo!

NAMES

Puunene is a name of a cinder cone near Paia. Paia is located in Hamakuapoko. Cod Fish Village got its name as the result of an argument. And it is very doubtful if many real Spaniards ever lived in the three HC&S villages that have Spanish as part of their names.

These are some of the strange things about the origin of some of HC&S Co. plantation village names.

For example, take Orpheum Village in Paia. True, it is near a movie house, but the name of this theater was never Orpheum. It is told that there was once an Orpheum in Lower Paia and another in Wailuku— all miles from Orpheum Village. And it has not been very helpful to learn that Orpheum is a Greek word meaning house of Orpheus, an ancient poet and musician.

It is fairly obvious how villages such as Store, Mill, Skill, School, Hospital, Dairy, Hawaiian, and Russian got their names.

Also, several villages derived their names from well-known men who lived on Maui before the turn of the century. Spreckelsville was named for Claus Spreckels, the one time "Sugar King". Spreckels founded one of the plantations which eventually became the HC&S of today. However, the Spreckels family no longer has any sugar interests in the Islands.

Young Hee, Sam Sing, and Afong were old-time field lunas who gave their names to the villages where their work gangs lived. McGerrow Village was named after Billy McGerrow who for many years worked in the HC&S Main Office.

Alabama Village received its name because a party of American Negroes who came to work on the plantation once lived there. Possibly they came from Alabama.

A few plantation villages were also known only by numbers.

Pukalani means gateway to heaven. This name was given to the Kula highway project in the early 30's and evidently refers to the idea that Kula is heavenly. No one seems to think that Pukalani may possibly have a more unfortunate literal meaning.

Kihei means shoulder cape, the type usually worn by kings and chiefs in olden times. It is said that the famous feather capes worn by Kamehameha and others were made at Kihei. Keahua means mound. Keahua Village was on a slight hill, but nothing to really suggest the name mound. The village was phased out when New Kahului was established.

Many, many years ago two plantation employees at Spreckelsville got into a name-calling argument. One of the men was a newly arrived Portuguese from the old country. The other man called him a cod fish, referring, no doubt, to the salt cod fish which was the staple food of the early Portuguese immigrants. And the name stuck.

When the present Puunene Mill was under construction, the project was often referred to as the new Spreckelsville Mill. However, at the laying of the corner stone, H. P. Baldwin, manager of the plantation, announced that the new mill would be called Puunene. Eventually the entire area around the mill came to be known as Puunene.

Actually, Puunene means goose hill and is the name of a small volcanic cinder cone between Spreckelsville and Paia. The original Puunene is gone because the cinders from the cone were used on many road projects and to build airstrips early in World War II.

Paia is the ancient name for this spot. Paia actually lies within the boundaries of Hamakuapoko, the district which runs from Kuiaha on the East to about the Maui Country Club on the West, and from the sea to the top of Haleakala. Hamakua is the Hawaiian word indicating a windward direction or Northeast. Poko means little. Hamakuapoko means the little Hamakua, to distinguish it from Hamakualoa, the big Hamakua.

MAUI TIME

Prior to World War I, every Maui plantation had its own time and blew its mill whistle accordingly. Kahului Railroad ran on another time. And "central" gave out over the phone yet another "correct time." Vestiges of this time mess persisted until 1948.

In 1916 you might have left Puunene for Lahaina at 2:30 p.m. and, according to Lahaina clocks, arrived at 2:15 p.m. The reverse trip could make the unwary very late.

Plantation time was adjusted frequently to take advantage of every instant of daylight. Because of mountains and the sun's rising in the east, Paia clocks sometimes were up to half an hour ahead of those at Puunene. In turn, Puunene clocks sometimes were a full hour ahead of Lahaina clocks.

A common question to ask, "Is that plantation time or central time?" but time marched on regardless.

TALES OF KAHULUI

Kahului means "the gathering place". This name became attached to the area in 1790 when Kamehameha landed a fleet of over a thousand war canoes there as part of his successful invasion of Central Maui. His choice of this "gathering place" was probably something of a surprise to Maui's defender, Kalanikupule, as there were many other safer and more usual landing places. The truth is, Kahului is centrally located, but it is not a natural haven from storm and wind. For almost a century engineers have been trying to make Kahului into an adequate harbor.

Before 1870, Kahului was little more than a sand bar separating swampy Kanaha Pond from the sea. Kanaha covered the old location of the A&B Lumber Yard, the Fairgrounds, and surrounding areas. As a harbor, Kahului had but one natural advantage: there was a narrow break in the coral which allowed ships to anchor inside the reef. Coral grows only in salt water. The break was caused by fresh water from the Waikapu River which at one time emptied into Kahului Bay.

Serious disadvantages included: an anchorage exposed to the full force of the trade winds, very little deep water, and a heavy surge. Moreover, Kahului is notorious for tidal waves. Possibly the worst was in 1883 at the time of the Krakatoa eruption. It is said a small schooner was carried inland and set down high and dry in the vicinity of the old Kahului School.

As early as 1840, there may have been a small jetty about where the Maui Palms is now located. Sailing vessels anchored off shore and passengers and freight were transferred in small boats. Large ships continued to anchor off shore until Pier 1 was built in 1923.

Steam navigation came to Hawaii in the 1860's and in 1872. The Wilder Steamship Co. built a good landing and freight crane at Kahului. The Wilders also operated a store in the wharf-shed.

The building of Maui's first railroad line, connecting Wailuku, Kahului, and Paia, was started by T. H. Hobron in 1879. When the job was completed in 1881, Kahului Railroad Co. was incorporated. Three years later, the Wilders acquired Hobron's railroad interest and expanded their business to include lightering cargoes and selling lumber.

Around 1877, Claus Spreckels built his own facilities at Kahului to handle HC&S shipping. Included was an HC&S store and office.

Friction developed with the Wilders in 1897. Because of HC&S land holdings, Spreckels was in a position to shut off Kahului Railroad from the waterfront—which he proceeded to do. The Wilders then started legal proceedings based on the railroad's being a public utility. Spreckels countered by organizing his own utility, Maui Railroad & Steamship Co., and turned HC&S land ringing Kahului over to it.

At this juncture, control of HC&S passed from Spreckels to the Alexander & Baldwin interests. However, Maui Railroad & Steamship Co., being a separate corporation, still was under Spreckels' control and he shut off both HC&S and Kahului Railroad from the waterfront. HC&S was forced to buy out both Spreckels and the Wilders in 1899. Thereafter all railroad and port facilities were assigned to Kahului Railroad Co.

In the legal vacuum prior to 1899, something like a squatter's town grew up. Conditions were very unsanitary. Serious bubonic plague broke out in 1900 and, to control the epidemic, Kahului was burned to the ground. Rebuilding followed, and modern Kahului may be said to date from 1906 with the opening of Maui's first bank, in the new two-story Masonic Building. It was also in 1906 that Kahului Railroad started the east breakwater and the harbor was dredged for the first time. Fill from the operation was used to form the land which is now the main business section.

The first wharf was built in 1910 to accommodate the S.S. Claudine, queen of the Inter-island fleet. Inter-island passengers to Maui could, for the first time, step directly ashore. The Claudine Wharf was damaged during the tidal wave of 1923. Pier 2 was built in 1928 on the same site.

Until 1910, private money had financed most of the Kahului improvements. After the completion of the Claudine Wharf, Kahului Railroad transferred the harbor and breakwater to the Federal Government. The first big Federal project was Pier 1 in 1923. There was extensive dredging at this time, and the area presently devoted to oil and molasses tanks was built with fill.

Possibly the largest ship ever to anchor off shore in Kahului Harbor was the British battleship HMS Capetown in 1922. It is said that among a group of young British officers who failed to get back from a party in Lahaina before the Capetown sailed to Honolulu was Albert Windsor, Duke of York, later King George VI of England.

In a further effort to make Kahului an all-weather port, the west breakwater was constructed in 1931. The first bulk sugar plant in the world was built at Kahului in 1941—in time for the start of World War II. Kahului was the scene of naval action on December 15 and again on December 30, 1941. A Japanese sub marine surfaced off Kahului and lobbed shells into the town. Fortunately none exploded. However, a smokestack at the Maui Pine cannery was damaged and holes were shot through the wharf-shed at Pier 1.

KAHULUI - THE DREAM THAT CAME TRUE

From barren sand hills, covered with kiawe, there has arisen a modern city of fee simple homes, bought at prices that would make an Oahu home buyer pale with envy.

It is "Dream City", grown beyond the most optimistic hopes of 1948, when Asa F. Baldwin, then manager of Hawaiian Commercial & Sugar Company first announced plans for the construction of "Greater Kahului," a modern town of fee simple homes built on ample ground for family gardens and outdoor living area, and a modern shopping center.

Building a model town on Maui was an old dream of Frank Baldwin and his brother Harry. The plan was actually formulated in 1947 to give HC&S employees an opportunity to own their own attractively priced homes in a model community. To promote a balanced community rather than just a company town, houses and lots were also sold to the public. Actual building started in 1949.

For the first time in any major town planning in the Islands, the street plan was set up to take full advantage of exposure to the trade winds. More than 300 acres was set aside for schools, parks, playgrounds, and some 30 acres for churches, clubs and other religious, public and semi-public organizations.

And prices? In the first six increments, the cost to an HC&S employee for a house and lot was as low as $6,600! And the highest was just $9,200.

"Dream City" is a successful demonstration of the friendly mingling of people of all races and creeds. The young bank employee lives alongside of a tractor driver from the plantation . . . and usually after work hours and on weekends, both can be seen talking politics, or baseball, between sessions with the lawnmower. It is probably safe to say that there are more orchid lathe houses and gardens of exotic plants in "Dream City" than in any other residential area anywhere. People have justified F. F. and Harry Baldwins' faith in them by taking great pride in their own homes.

At the time the original plan was announced, it was believed that development of the area would be spread over at least twenty-five years.

In an announcement in 1948, Asa Baldwin said:

"Our hope is for a modern community to provide progressively better housing and living for residents of central Maui. The sponsoring companies will have to put thousands and thousands of dollars into the enterprise. We know that investment in community welfare is good business for all of Maui.

"We will not let this project become a 'land speculation deal' in any respect. It cannot be rushed. It will take time. It must be given a natural growth . . . We hope that some day it will grow to become a city of 4,000 homes."

One important result of the success of this development is that it has made it possible for HC&S to raze older rental units, as more and more employees bought new homes of their own.

As you drive through the wide streets, past the neat lawns and gardens, the thought automatically leaps to mind—yes, here is indeed a dream come true.

THE REIGN OF THE SUGAR KING

Spreckelsville—a sleepy little village on the north shore of Maui—certainly gives no hint today of the history that was made there years ago. But the haole name, tossed into the heartland of Hawaii's sugar industry, with names like Kahului, Wailuku, Paia, made history. The man was Claus Spreckels—the sugar industry a babe-in-arms when he arrived in 1878.

Born in Hanover, Germany, Spreckels arrived in the United States in 1846 and began working for $14 a week as a grocery store clerk, later beginning his own grocery business. He purchased a California brewery in 1863 and already had enough assets to search around for an investment other than the brewery. When he chose a small sugar refinery in San Francisco, it was his beginning.

Spreckels arrived in Honolulu in 1878, the same year S. T. Alexander and Henry Baldwin completed the Hamakua ditch. Before his arrival, he had done more than accumulate assets, he had learned considerable about the sugar refinery business. And whether or not there was much aloha waiting, he brought ideas to Spreckelsville, Maui, never before tried.

His invention of a 24-hour process for refining sugar was an important one. Before it had taken nearly two weeks. In 1881 the first electric lights lit the sugar mill in Spreckelsville—five years before the royalty at Iolani Palace got electricity.

Captain T. H. Hobron, owner of Kahului Railroad at the time, ran an "alii special" carrying King Kalakaua, Dowager Queen Emma and Princess Ruth Keelikolani to view the mill at night—it was grinding cane at night—a sight never before seen in the islands.

It was at Spreckelsville where the first intra-plantation railroads were introduced for hauling . . . and where the first steam plow went to work in the cane fields. The first 5-roller mill in the Kingdom was set up there. And Claus Spreckels was not to be outdone if he could help it. He built a spectacular irrigation ditch. It ran 30 miles long, carried 50,000,000 gallons of water each day.

Spreckels' company, Hawaiian Commercial & Sugar Co., was founded in 1872 and termed "the largest, most modern in the world—40,000 acres of land, 25,000 of good cane land, 12,000 under cultivation."

Within the next ten years, he was buying nearly the entire crop of island raw sugar and he owned, or nearly owned, every company that touched Hawaiian sugar. Even Oceanic Steamship Co., which carried the crops across the Pacific, was his. And it was refined at a Spreckels-owned refinery on the coast, and the profits deposited in his own banking and agency houses in Honolulu.

From his Maui plantation, Spreckels returned to Honolulu and built a three-story mansion on a 17-acre tract on Punahou Street, makai of the academy. The $20,000 house was the scene of many political and social gatherings, and was as grandiose as most of his endeavors.

Spreckels looked to astrology for inspiration and guidance. One can scarcely conceive of a multi-millionaire "Sugar King" checking his daily horoscope before making a move, but his home near Punahou reflected it. On the ceiling of his showplace home were signs and symbols of the zodiac, and probably beneath them he sat and worried over whether Jupiter and Saturn were in their proper houses.

1886 was recorded as the turning point in the Spreckels story— till then a story of success, profits, and more success. Under the direction of S. T. Alexander, a pool was formed of the independent Hawaiian plantations—those not already in the Spreckels net. Markets not under his control were found, and in 1893 HC&S was in trouble. A call to shareholders of HC&S for more money resulted in rejection.

Captain Hobron's Kahului Railroad Co. had been the prime mover of cane to the dock at Kahului. A five-acre patch of land, owned by Spreckels, was being used to effectively halt the flow of sugar out of Maui. It was crucial to the delivery of sugar to the port, and Spreckels refused to sell. In a move to avoid legal action, Spreckels formed his own railroad—Maui Railroad & Steamship Co.—became a public utility and moved to shut off both HC&S and Kahului Railroad.

Alexander and Baldwin became the principal shareholders of HC&S in 1898 and Spreckels left the islands for San Francisco. At the same time A&B began action in California to release the port blockade at Kahului. In 1899 HC&S purchased the railroad company stock for $60,000 and its merchandise for $43,610 and gained control of both Kahului Railroad and the port facilities.

In 1898, local aloha was running thin. After finding an unpleasant drawing and threatening note nailed to his front gate, Spreckels sailed away the next noon. News slips of the day report he hadn't made the beds or washed the breakfast dishes before his hasty departure. At the dock he swore: "I'll not return till grass grows on Fort Street."

MEMORABLE YEARS

1848

Haliimaile Plantation is organized. It extends from just below the present Paia Mill mauka to the present Grove Ranch area between Sunnyside Road and Kailua Gulch. Later this plantation was known as Brewer Plantation, then Union Plantation (during the Civil War) and finally, Grove Ranch Plantation. It merged with Paia Plantation in 1889.

1851

Paholei Mill of Haliimaile Plantation starts operation. Ruins can still be seen. The first sugar centrifugal was installed here.

1853

The Kingdom of Hawaii sets aside the ahupuaa of Hamakuapoko for the Board of Education, over 5,000 acres. The Board deeded Hamakuapoko to the Trustees of Oahu College in 1860 and, in turn, they sold it the following year to the Haiku Sugar Co. The area was larger than the company could use and parcels were sold from time to time. Captain William Bush bought 559 acres at Sunnyside in 1865. Much of the early corporate history of predecessor companies centers around the mergers and purchases which reunited the original ahupuaa of Hamakuapoko.

1857

East Maui Plantation with its mill at Kaluanui is organized by H. A. Spencer. It was also known as Kaluanui Plantation and was purchased by Haiku Sugar Co. in 1886.

1858

Haiku Sugar Co. is organized by George Douglas and continued as a major plantation until 1921 when it merged to form Maui Agricultural Co., Ltd.

1861

Mill is built at Haiku. The remains of this mill are still visible beside the Hana Highway. Sugar from this mill was shipped from Maliko bay. The East Maui Seminary for Hawaiian Girls (later known as Maunaolu Seminary) is established at Makawao.

1868

First Japanese immigrants arrive.

1869

H. P. Baldwin borrows $900 to join S. T. Alexander in buying the Bush Ranch, the first unit of the operation which eventually was to be incorporated as Paia Plantation and was known at various times as Sam T. Alexander & Co., Haleakala Sugar Co., and Alexander & Baldwin Plantation. East Maui Plantation Company agrees to grind cane for S. T. Alexander and others. The East Maui Seminary burns and is rebuilt.

1870

Robert Hind, in agreement with S. T. Alexander and H. P. Baldwin, builds a mill to grind their cane on a 50-50 basis. This mill is at Paliuli, present site of the Makawao Union Church. Sugar is shipped from Kuau to Honolulu, then trans-shipped to the Mainland. A meeting house is located at Makawao, present site of the Makawao Cemetery. Catholic Church is built at Kuau at the present site of the Kuau Catholic Cemetery.

1871

S. T. Alexander is appointed manager of Haiku Sugar Co. J. M. Alexander Seaside Farm is located at Kuau. The farm was purchased by Paia Plantation in 1884.

1872

S. T. Alexander and H. P. Baldwin buy out Robert Hind. Hawaiian Commercial Co. is organized by Claus Spreckels. The village near the mill is named Spreckelsville. The present Hana Highway crosses a corner of the area formerly occupied by the mill.

1876

H. P. Baldwin loses his right arm in an accident at Paliuli Mill. A Reciprocity Treaty is signed between the Hawaiian Kingdom and the United States. This gives Hawaii the advantage of duty-free sugar. A water lease is secured from the Hawaiian Kingdom for water rights in East Maui. The ditch has to be completed in two years or all improvements revert to the government.

1877

Haiku Sugar Co. is offered to Claus Spreckels for $500,000 but the offer is not accepted. Later in the year water from the Hamakua Ditch reaches the Haiku fields east of Maliko.

1878

Claus Spreckels secures a lease to water rights below and beyond the Hamakua Ditch. If the Hamakua Ditch is not completed on time, he will get that too. The ditch is completed to Maliko Gulch but workers, will not go down the sides of the gulch to work on the pipe. H. P. Baldwin's arm is not yet completely healed, but he goes down a rope into the gulch one-handed and, by his example, encourages the men into going ahead with the work. The ditch is completed just in time. The first Portuguese immigrants arrive. C. H. Dickey introduced first telephone on Maui at Haiku. By 1883 there was a telephone line from Haiku to Hamakuapoko, Paia, Kahului and Waihee.

1880

Haiku Sugar Co. builds a new mill at Hamakuapoko. The Hind Mill at Paliuli is replaced by a new mill at Paia in the present location.

1881

Kahului Railroad Co. is incorporated. During the next five years the railroad is extended in Wailuku and Lower Paia. When the Lower Paia line is finished, the Kuau landing is abandoned and all sugar is shipped through Kahului directly to the Mainland. An agreement is reached to grind Grove Ranch cane at Paia Mill and the Paholei mill is closed. The one and only contingent of Norwegian immigrants arrive.

1882

HC&S is incorporated as a California corporation. The Spreckels ditch is completed below the Hamakua Ditch. An organization, the forerunner of the Hawaiian Sugar Planters' Association, is started in Honolulu.

1883

S. T. Alexander is forced to resign as manager of Haiku Sugar Co. because of ill health. H. P. Baldwin succeeds him. E. M. Walsh is manager of Paia. Paia Plantation is incorporated. Previously it was a personal partnership between S. T. Alexander and H. P. Baldwin.

1884

Haiku Sugar Co. abandons Haiku Mill and all planting east of Maliko.

1885

H. L. Dodge is president of HC&S. Total assets are $3,675,000 but the company is burdened by a $1,100,000 bonded debt. First HC&S hospital is opened at Spreckelsville.

1886

S. T. Alexander takes lead in forming pool of most Hawaiian plantations. The pool contracts with the American Refinery to handle their raw sugar. The Wilder Steamship Co., forerunner of Inter-Island, buys Kahului Railroad.

1887

Hawaiian Constitution is adopted. H. P. Baldwin is elected to the Legislature as a candidate of the Reform Party (in favor of a constitutional monarchy.)

1890

First pineapples at Haiku are planted by D. D. Baldwin. Claus Spreckels proposes consolidation of HC&S with Paia and Haiku plantations. This does not go through because it would mean assuming bonded indebtedness of HC&S.

1891

McKinley Tariff Act removes duty on Cuban sugar and the price goes down to $50 a ton. Claus Spreckels makes a deal with the Eastern Sugar Trust and the American Refinery becomes part of the Western Sugar Refining Co., which Spreckels controls.

1893

HC&S goes broke and stockholders are called upon for an assessment. Many refuse to "throw good money after bad" and lose their investments in the company. The Baldwin Home for Boys and Men at Kalaupapa, Molokai, is financed by H. P. Baldwin. He also rebuilds his father's old Wainee Church at Lahaina.

1894

The Republic of Hawaii is established. H. P. Baldwin serves as delegate to the founding convention. The Alexander & Baldwin agency is started in San Francisco and represents Haiku and Paia plantations. HC&S installs it first pumping plant near the present Central Power Plant.

1895

Hawaiian Sugar Planters' Association is organized and its Experiment Station is started. H. A. Baldwin succeeds his father as manager of Haiku Sugar Co.

1896

First resident physician, Dr. L. A. Sabey, is employed by HC&S. Brig "Lurline," a small sailing vessel, is listed as an asset of HC&S. First Paia Store is built.

1897

California & Hawaiian Sugar Refining Co. is organized. Alexander & Baldwin, Ltd., opens offices in Honolulu. Spreckels forms the Maui Railroad and Steamship Co. and, since HC&S owns all the Kahului waterfront, he is able to blockade Kahului Railroad from access to the shore.

1898

Annexation of Hawaii to United States on August 12, 1898. But, Henry Baldwin innocently jumped the gun. He threw a big annexation luau—with practically all Maui attending—at Haiku Plantation on August 10.

During the celebration the American flag was proudly raised over the plantation's Hamakuapoko mill. Meanwhile, the annexation date had been changed from the 10th to the 12th. But news traveled by ship in those days so Baldwin didn't receive word of the change in time. Thus, in a sense, Maui became the first Hawaiian Island to join the United States.

First Spanish immigrants. Edward Pollitz, a San Francisco broker, buys control of HC&S and is elected president. Total assets at this time are $3,942,000 but Pollitz authorizes improvements that will nearly double the size of the crop. Pollitz sells control to Alexander & Baldwin, Ltd., and H. P. Baldwin is elected president. Paia Plantation completes installation of Lower Paia pumps and installs a new nine-roller mill and engines. A hospital is opened at Paia and Dr. Aiken, soon to be succeeded by Dr. McConkey, is resident physician. The hospital buildings were later used for the Paia Club House and more recently the East Maui Community Association had their headquarters here. Kihei Plantation is organized with W. F. Pogue as manager. Maunaolu Seminary burns for the second time.

1899

First automobile on Maui belongs to H. P. Baldwin. HC&S buys Maui Railroad and Steamship Co. and Kahului Railroad to end blockade. R. W. Filler is manager of Kahului Railroad. W. J. Lowrie is manager of HC&S. Construction of Lowrie Ditch starts. HC&S agrees to grind Kihei Plantation cane. Haiku Sugar Co. starts first kindergarten. Large immigration of Portuguese, Japanese, Germans, and Italians. Kihei Plantation drills two wells and builds store and wharf at Kihei.

1900

Bubonic plague in Kahului town and town is burned to destroy rats. Jump cane fire burns 575 acres at HC&S. Portable track is laid to Paia and some of the cane is ground by Paia and Hamakuapoko mills. HC&S., Paia and Haiku plantations, change railroads to same standard, three-foot gauge. HC&S buys four new locomotives. Lowrie Ditch is completed. Orders are placed for new Puunene Mill to replace the Spreckelsville Mill. Large immigrations of Japanese, Negroes, and Puerto Ricans. Lower Paia Depot burns. Maunaolu Seminary is rebuilt by H. P. Baldwin in present location. Maui Planters' Association is organized. Maui News commences publication.

Lowrie resigns and H. P. Baldwin becomes both president and manager of HC&S. Puunene Mill starts grinding with one nine-roller mill. Second mill from Spreckelsville is being installed. Brig "Lurline" no longer listed as an asset. Fuel oil commences to replace coal.

1903

Organic Act limits land holdings of new corporations to 1,000 acres. For this reason, five companies are formed, just under 1,000 acres each—Kailua Plantation, Kalialinui Plantation, Kula Plantation, Makawao Plantation and Pulehu Plantation. With Paia Plantation and Haiku Sugar Co., a co-partnership, is organized to allow joint operation of a sugar mill and other facilities. The co-partnership is called Maui Agricultural Co. and H. A. Baldwin is manager. All seven companies were merged into Maui Agricultural Co., Ltd. in 1921 when 1,000-acre limitation was repealed. A wing is added to Spreckelsville Hospital and X-ray machine is added. First Korean immigration. Kihei Pump 3 building burns.

1904

Koolau Ditch is completed. M.A. Co. orders equipment for new Paia Mill to be built on site of old Paia Mill. Plan to close Hamakuapoko Mill. S. T. Alexander dies following accident while touring in Africa.

1905

Paia Mill completed except for moving machinery from Hamakuapoko. Kahului Railroad line relocated from Lower to Upper Paia. American Ship "Spartan" loaded with coal is wrecked on reef off Spreckelsville.

1906

F. F. Baldwin succeeds father as manager of HC&S. First Filipino immigration. Hamakuapoko Mill is closed. East Maui land turned over to forest reserve. Kahului Railroad builds east breakwater, first at Kahului, and harbor is dredged.

1907

HC&S and Wailuku Sugar Co. build new Waihee Ditch. Rubber trees planted at Nahiku.

1908

East Maui Irrigation Co., Ltd. is organized jointly by HC&S and M.A. Co. to manage the ditches and to divide East Maui water. New Paia School is built, previous school was at Kaheka. Kihei Plantation is merged with HC&S. First Puunene Store (A&B Store, Kahului now stands on site) is opened. Lime Kiln at Paia starts operation.

1909

New Paia Hospital built. Large numbers of Russian, Portuguese and Filipino immigrants arrive.

1910

Epidemic of smallpox among Filipinos. Paia Store and M.A. Co. office burn down and the present buildings are constructed to replace them. Kahului Harbor and breakwater are turned over to the Federal Government.

1911

H. P. Baldwin dies and F. F. Baldwin becomes president and manager of HC&S. H. A. Baldwin becomes president and manager of M.A. Co. Fred Baldwin Memorial Home for old men is built.

1912

Extensive home building and road paving is underway. Villages improved.

1913

New Puunene Hospital is completed and Spreckelsville Hospital closed. Nahiku rubber plantation is abandoned because of drop in rubber prices. Kahului Railroad completes trestle over Maliko and extends line to Haiku. Maui High School opens.

1914

New Haiku Ditch is completed. HC&S installs first sand filters to purify water for drinking. New Kahului Store (present A&B Commercial Co. main office) is built. Kauhikoa Ditch is completed. First Boy Scout troop on Maui at Paia.

1916

In January Maui suffers worst kona storm on record. In Iao 30 homes are washed away and 13 people are killed. New Puunene Club House and cottages are built. M.A. Co erects a cement plant at the Lime kiln in Lower Paia. First Maui County Fair.

1917

New stone Makawao Union Church is built. World War I draft seriously reduces work force. New HC&S main office built. M.A. Co. builds distillery to make alcohol from molasses because of shortage of kerosene, gasoline, etc. Wheat flour also is scarce because of the war and M.A. Co. plants corn at Haiku. For a time the Haiku corn flour mill supplies all the Territory. The Kahului Lyceum Theater burns down. HC&S is electrifying old steam pumps.

1918

HC&S spends $3,l45 on autos, trucks, and tractors, first time this equipment appears on the books as a separate item.

1919

Influenza epidemic—over 2,000 cases and seven deaths. HC&S builds theater at Spreckelsville and a Filipino club house. Record all-time high price for sugar, May 19, $471.40 a ton.

1920

Electrification of villages starts. Many playgrounds, athletic fields and theaters constructed. Maui County Free Library becomes major project of Maui Women's Club. Japanese strike.

1922

H. A. Baldwin is Hawaii Delegate to Congress.

1923

Tidal wave at Kahului causes $1,500,000 damage. HC&S builds new store at Spreckelsville. Manufacture of alcohol is abandoned with return of low gasoline prices. Pier 1 at Kahului is built.

1924

Paia Armory is built. Territory purchases Claudine Wharf at Kahului.

1926

HC&S is incorporated in Hawaii, replacing former California corporation. All East Maui lands of both HC&S and M.A. Co. are deeded to East Maui Irrigation Co. Church of the Holy Rosary is built at Paia.

1927

HC&S completes Well 7 with 40 million gallons per day capacity—one of the largest deep wells in the world.

1928

Pier 2 at Kahului is completed. Spreckelsville Store and nearby bean mill burn and store is rebuilt.

1929

Sewer systems are being built in various plantation villages. Haleakala Pineapple Co. is formed by H. A. Baldwin and S. A. Baldwin. Inter-Island Airways starts operation.

1930

Record rainstorm. Up to 10.25 inches fall in one hour, November 28, doing tremendous damage to older ditches. Well 1 at Spreckelsville, last of HC&S steam pumps, is abandoned.

1931

Present breakwaters at Kahului completed.

1932

Maui Pineapple Co. incorporated to take over Haleakala Pineapple Co. and pineapple department of M.A. Co. J. P. Foster is making alpha cellulose from bagasse experimentally at M.A. Co.

1933

Tractor plowing replaces steam plows at HC&S.

1934

Congress sets first domestic quotas on sugar production.

1935

F. F. Baldwin Park at Puunene is built. M.A. Co. abandons steam plows. Kahului Railroad replaces passenger trains with buses.

1937

HC&S starts first sizable mechanical harvesting. M.A. Co. is making white sugar. Filipino strike.

1938

Paia Gym is built. Severe earthquake causes great deal of damage. Asa F. Baldwin becomes assistant manager of M.A. Co. Puunene Airport is under construction.

1940

New high school at Wailuku is named in honor of H. P. Baldwin. Construction of Puunene Naval Air Station starts.

1941

New Puunene Store is built at Kahului and bulk sugar plant is under construction. December 7, Pearl Harbor and the United States is at war. M.A. Co. sets aside 70 acres for victory gardens.

1942

Government takes 3,800 acres at Puunene and Kahului for air fields. Kahului is shelled twice by submarines. Milling is confined to daylight hours until blackout of mills is approved in April. First bulk sugar shipments.

1944

Almost half of electric power produced by HC&S is sold to Maui Electric Co. for military use.

1945

World War II ends. ILWU recognized as bargaining agent for hourly-rated employees. . Smallest crop in many years because of war. Puunene Community Association is formed.

1946

Asa F. Baldwin succeeds H. A. Baldwin as manager of M.A. Co. Later in the year H. A. Baldwin dies. Tidal wave strikes Islands with heavy damage and loss of life. Big sugar strike that ends with conversion of perquisites to cash pay. H. A. Baldwin Memorial Park is constructed and Supervisors' Club is organized.

1947

M.A. Co. converts to truck cane hauling. KMVI starts broadcasting.

1948

HC&S and M. A. Co. merge to form present plantation. F. F. Baldwin retains presidency but is succeeded by Asa F. Baldwin as manager. Plan for New Kahului is announced. Puunene Hospital is modernized and enlarged. First radio telephones are installed in field cars. East Maui Community Association is formed.

1949

Longshore strike and bulk sugar is stored in emergency facilities. Paia Hospital is closed and buildings are turned over to Maui Children's Home. New wing is added to Puunene office. Kahului Development Co. is organized. Puunene railroads abandoned.

1950

First unit of New Kahului is occupied. Plantation stores and Kahului Railroad Merchandise Department merged to form A&B Commercial Co. Maunaolu Seminary, closed during war, reopens as junior college.

1951

A&B Super Market opens. First traffic light on Maui is installed in Kahului.

1952

November 4 tidal wave floods Kahului. Central Maui Memorial Hospital is opened.

1955

Maui gets two television stations on Haleakala. Island-wide dial telephone system completed.

1956

Puunene Hospital is closed and services consolidated with those of Central Maui Memorial.

1957

Tidal wave hits March 9; little serious damage. HC&S celebrates Diamond Jubilee April 3.

1960

Frank Fowler Baldwin dies on February 6, 1960, marking the end of an era on the plantation. Much loved, he guided HC&S from just another sugar plantation on Maui in 1906 to become one of the largest cane sugar producers in the world. Announcement was made in December of the resignation of Asa F. Baldwin as manager of HC&S.

WITNESS TO A CENTURY OF SERVICE
HISTORY OF MAKAWAO UNION CHURCH DATES FROM MAUI'S MISSIONARY DAYS.

"I, Lot Kamehameha, Minister of the Interior, with the advice and consent of the King and Privy Council, by virtue of the power vested in me by Section 1142 of the Civil Code of the Hawaiian Islands, hereby grant this Charter to N. F. Sayer, Gustavus M. Spencer, and Thomas H. Hobron, and their successors elected as hereafter provided, who are hereby constituted a Corporation and body politic who shall have perpetual continuance under the name and style of the Makawao Church and Congregation..."

Thus, the future King Kamehameha V on April 20, 1861, chartered in his own handwriting the church which we know now as Makawao Union.

The church was an outgrowth of religious meetings held by the Reverend Jonathan S. Green in his home at Pookela, Makawao, in 1857. These services were conducted in English, rather than Hawaiian, for the benefit of the "foreigners" in the community.

Mr. Green arrived with his wife Theodosia in Hawaii on March 30, 1828, with the third company of missionaries. Bearing the title given to all the missionaries, he was known as Father Alaska, San Francisco, Hilo, Lahaina, and Wailuku. In 1843, however, he left the service of the American Board because "the relations the Board sustains to American slavery are not right in the sight of God."

Father Green then accepted an invitation of Hawaiians in Makawao to be their pastor. They provided only a grass hut, but Father Green worked in the fields and as a carpenter helped the people establish the first self-supporting church in Hawaii. The stone building they erected at Pookela still stands.

After Theodosia died in 1859, Father Green took a furlough on the Mainland. During his year and a half away, the Reverend C. B. Andrews carried on his work. Father Andrews had arrived in 1844 with the eleventh company of missionaries.

Father Andrews organized the girls' school which was forerunner of today's Maunaolu College. He also applied for and received from Lot Kamehameha the first charter for Makawao Church and, thus, commenced the continuing close association of Maunaolu with Makawao Union. The church was built at the present location of Makawao Cemetery—indeed, the earliest graves were in the church yard. The building was dedicated on March 3, 186l, and was used until 1889. Around 1900 it was still standing.

Father Green returned to Makawao with his second wife Asenath in 1863 and was soon back at work as pastor of Pookela Church and the new "Foreign" Church.

Henry Perrine Baldwin, son of Dwight Baldwin of the fourth company of missionaries, married Miss Emily Alexander at Wailuku on April 5, 1870. Their first home was at Sunnyside, and they both became active in the Makawao Church. Among other things, Mr. Baldwin played the organ for services. Twice on rainy Sundays, Father Green and Mr. Baldwin were the only ones there. The first time, Father Green gave his sermon as usual. The next, he and Mr. Baldwin discussed the plight of the lepers on Molokai.

Mr. Baldwin, in partnership with his brother-in-law Samuel Alexander, had bought the former Bush Ranch at Sunnyside and converted it to a sugar cane plantation. All their money, plus all they could borrow, was invested in the enterprise. The outlook was grim when their efforts were threatened by a prolonged drought. One day when things were desperate, it is said that Mr. Baldwin got off his horse and prayed for rain. He promised that if the plantation were saved he would always return a portion of his earnings for God's work.

The rains came and Mr. Baldwin's promise has been kept, even to the third and fourth generation—as churches and schools on Maui, and the settlement at Kalaupapa, Molokai, can testify.

In 1870, Robert Hind built a small sugar mill at Paliuli on the edge of Rainbow Gulch. By agreement, he processed cane grown by Alexander and Baldwin. On March 28, 1876, Mr. Baldwin was testing the clearance between the mill rollers when his fingers were caught and his right arm was drawn into the mill. He was almost killed before the engine could be reversed. He was taken to the home of the mill engineer next door, where his arm was amputated.

At the time, the partners were engaged in building a ditch to bring East Maui water to cane west of Maliko Gulch. Rights to the water depended upon completing the project on time. When the project reached Maliko, the workers were reluctant to go down the precipice. Mr. Baldwin, hardly recovered from his amputation, went down the rope. When the workers saw him negotiate the rope with only one arm, they returned to the job and the project was completed on time.

It was in this same year, 1876, that Mr. Baldwin joined with Father Green, Mr. Spencer, and the Reverend James Alexander to apply for a second church charter. The name now was the Foreign Religious Society of Makawao, and James Alexander was hired to help Father Green, who was in failing health. Father Green died on January 5, 1878. He was 82.

The Reverend T. H. Rouse was called and served as pastor from 1878 until 1885.

His son preached for several months and then the Reverend James Alexander helped out until the arrival of the Reverend Mr. Lounsberry. Mr. Lounsberry was a bachelor who disliked the tradewinds, hated flowers on the pulpit, and "amused" Mrs. Baldwin by saying there would surely be a black sheep among her boys. He had ribbons sewed on his hat for tying under his chin to keep it on and, all in all, it is little wonder that he soon left. He was replaced in 1886 by the Reverend T. H. Gulick. Mr. Gulick served until 1893.

Meanwhile, Alexander and Baldwin enterprises flourished. By 1888 Mr. Baldwin was looking for ways to keep his promise regarding the support of churches. For one thing, he saw that the Makawao minister had one of those new-fangle telephones. Then suddenly, the church trustees were asked whether they would accept a new church nearer the center of population.

There was much discussion and it was finally agreed that the site of the Paliuli Mill, which had been closed since 1880, would be acceptable. The new building cost $8,000 and was given with the site, debt-free to the congregation by Mr. Baldwin. It was constructed on the original mill foundation. The fine frame building was dedicated on March 10, 1889. The weather vane was donated by J. B. Atherton. The bell was a gift of Castle and Cooke.

It was decided in 1890 to extend the back of the church for a choir loft and pipe organ. According to church records, it cost 50 cents a week to pay someone to hand-pump the new organ during services. This same organ was later used for years at the old Kahului Union Church.

Stained glass windows were another addition. These were later reinstalled along with several new ones in the present stone building.

Other expenditures covered the purchase of 60 folding chairs, a picket fence, and a hitching post. The janitor received $50 a year. The books also show that for many years the minister received an extra $300 to preach at Pookela. Also, a new church was organized and built at Haiku by the Makawao Religious Society. The ladies met on

February 20, 1889, to organize the Ladies Aid Society for all "ladies interested in the benevolent work of the church."

In 1893 a Dr. Frazer supplied the church for a few months after Mr. Gulick left. Then the well-remembered Reverend Edward G. Beckwith came to Maui and served actively until 1905. He continued on emeritus status until his death in 1909.

It was about this time that Paia Community House was built adjacent to the church. To finance the project, Clarence White of Haiku spearheaded a public subscription drive. An enlarged stage, dressing rooms, and the kitchen wing were later additions. Until other facilities were provided on the Island, the Paia Community House was in almost continuous use by various groups for the presentation of plays, operettas, school graduations, concerts, lectures, and dances.

The Reverend William Rice supplied for a few months in 1905 and then the Reverend B. V. Bazata served until 1907. He was followed by the Reverend E. B. Turner.

Mr. Turner often reminisced about playing polo with the Baldwin boys and how he and Dr. Stoddard climbed to the top of Iao Needle. He served through 1911. It was he who preached the memorial service for Henry Perrine Baldwin.

After Mr. Baldwin's death, his heirs decided to erect a new church in his memory. By September 2, 1917, the new stone building was ready to be dedicated. The name was now officially, Makawao Union Church.

The new building was about the same size as the frame building, for it also stood on the original Paliuli Mill foundation. There was a new pipe organ in memory of Leslie and Jared Baldwin, sons of Mr. and Mrs. Harry Baldwin. A baptismal font was donated by Hawaiian and Japanese friends.

The Reverend R. B. Dodge served for a few months in 1912, but it was the Reverend A. Craig Bowdish who preached the last sermon in the old church and the first in the new. He continued as pastor until 1921 with one year's leave to serve with the YMCA during World War I.

A new parsonage was built at Sunnyside for Mr. Bowdish and in 1961 it was turned over to Maunaolu College.

The Reverend Augustine Jones, an impressive speaker, served from 1921 to 1925. He was followed by the Reverend W. E. Rowan, a Methodist from Canada. Mr. Rowan's tenure of 20 years was longest in the church's century-old history.

A severe earthquake in 1938 damaged the Paia Community House, moving it off its foundations. The church building, however, escaped practically unscathed.

During the trying years of World War II, Makawao Union rendered service by furnishing a church home for servicemen stationed on Maui.

After the war, the Reverend C. K. Imbrie brought renewed vigor to the church in early 1947. Then the Reverend Augustus H. Griffing carried on until the end of 1956. Dr. William Fry supplied for several months until the coming of Dr. Hudson Pitman, who rendered loving ministry until his health failed in June 1956. He was followed by Rev. B. Ross Cleeland.

When the stone church was dedicated, Harry Baldwin, eldest son of Henry Perrine Baldwin, gave the principal address. He said of Makawao Union that it was built...

"To provide a permanent meeting house where the people of this community, his friends and our friends, and their children and children's children, and future comers, can gather for the purpose of upholding and improving the moral and religious standing of the community for generations to come. And it is our hope that this church will always be a potent factor for good and a blessing to Makawao and Maui."

MAUI AND THE CIVIL WAR

Maui was less remote from the alarms of the Civil War than geography would indicate. For one thing, practically every missionary in Hawaii was from New England and had close friends and relatives in the Union army. Missionary prayers were for the North. On the other hand, the court of Kamehameha IV was pro-British and joined with the upper British classes in their outspoken Southern sympathies.

At first, a quick Confederate victory and permanent dissolution of the Union were freely predicted in the Islands. But there was apprehension too. It was stated as a fact that California planned to become a separate nation and that it would seek forceful annexation of the Hawaiian Islands. Within a month of Fort Sumter, wild rumors circulated through Lahaina that a Confederate privateer was operating in the Pacific with orders to sink every Yankee whaling ship on sight. What if such a ship should attack the whalers which made Lahaina their winter headquarters?

Then, the market price of sugar went soaring upward and the infant Hawaiian sugar industry had its first taste of real success. The price of sugar was high because the war had cut off Louisiana sugar plantations from markets north of the Mason and Dixon line. Hawaiian sugar that once went to San Francisco was soon dispatched by any vessel available around the Horn to New York and Boston. Many new plantations, sugar mills, and supporting businesses were established at this time.

What was Maui like in 1861. Very few buildings used in that period are still standing and in use. Others are represented by ruins and rubble. Most were thatched houses and have vanished completely.

The population was principally Hawaiian, plus a few Haoles and Chinese. Individual towns and plantations were not connected by roads. Although a foot trail called the King's Way circled the island, the usual method of travel from place to place was by sea. There was not a single foot or paved street anywhere. In fact, there was really no road between Kahului and Wailuku. Wagons and carriages were driven along the beach.

Lahaina was still the leading community of Maui in 1861. Although it was but little used after 1858, the King maintained his palace at Lahaina as a summer residence even after the capitol had been removed to Honolulu. The palace was a two-story building on a brick foundation. The grounds which occupied the area presently devoted to Kamehameha III School, contained a number of smaller guest houses and out-buildings. From the sea, the palace was still the most prominent feature of the town at the time of the Civil War. For the most part, it was a community of grass houses.

Next to the palace was a fort on the site of the present courthouse and post office. By 1861 its cannons had long since been removed, but from its walls a curfew drum was still sounded every night. The beating of the drum was a signal for sailors to return to their ships.

There were fewer whaling ships wintering at Lahaina than there were in the 50's. Petroleum had been discovered in Pennsylvania and everywhere the cleaner kerosene lamp was replacing the smelly whale-oil lamp. Also, early in the Civil War a number of whalers were recalled to New Bedford. It was more profitable to carry cargoes or, perhaps, run the Union blockade of Confederate ports than to hunt whale.

But by and large, outfitting whaling ships was Lahaina's principal industry when the Civil War started. By its end, sugar had come into its own.

A wonder in 1861 was the first inter-island steamer Kilauea. It had been in operation for a year. Passengers could take the steamer to Maalaea and from there, there was a fair road to Wailuku. In addition to Lahaina, Maalaea and Kahakuloa, other so-called ports on Maui were Makena, Nahiku, Huelo, Maliko, and Waihee.

Small, unirrigated sugar plantations were in operation at Lahaina, Waikapu, Wailuku, Waihee, Ulupalakua, Kipahulu, Hana, Keanae, Nahiku, Huelo, Maliko, and Waihee.

During the Civil War, the plantation at Haliimaile was owned by a partnership composed of Dr. Gerret Judd, his son, and his son-in-law. Dr. Judd was a prominent missionary-physician. He resigned as a missionary to become principal court advisor to the king. He was so enthusiastic about the Northern cause that he named his company, Union Plantation. His mill at Paholei burned in 1864. The ruins may still be seen.

The land around Puunene was a complete desert. A great, barren stretch of sand and dust spread from Wailuku to Paia, except for a little cattle grazing land around the present location of Spreckelsville. It was not until the coming of irrigation and pumping projects in the 1870's that sugar cane could be grown in this area.

The first big problem presented by the Civil War was establishing the official neutrality of the Hawaiian Kingdom as a possible protection against raids by Confederate ships. The trouble was that an official declaration of neutrality would automatically recognize the Confederate States as a legitimate government. After much vacillation, and perhaps as a result of the early Southern victory at Bull Run, Kamehameha IV finally declared the neutrality of his kingdom. His proclamation went to great lengths to avoid naming the Confederate States of America but, nevertheless, he technically recognized the rebels.

The Honolulu missionary newspaper The Friend almost ignored the Civil War and the issue of slavery at the outset. This official and somewhat mealy-mouthed policy reflected the policy of the American Board of Foreign Missions, sponsors of the missionaries. Many missionaries working in Hawaii were irritated. Several, like Father Jonathan Green who founded Makawao Union Church, resigned because the Board refused to condemn slavery. This accounts for the fact that Makawao Union Church of Paia is today an independent Congregational church. In this it is unlike the majority of missionary-founded Congregational churches which are directly controlled by the Hawaiian Evangelical Association, modern successor to the American Board. It has been suggested that the American Board was influenced in its attitude at the start of the Civil War by the heavy financial support for the missionary effort that came from the people of the Southern States.

Toward the close of the Civil War, The Friend made up for its early silence. There were now strong anti-slavery articles in practically every issue of the publication. The South was castigated repeatedly. Lincoln's greatness was given full recognition. His assassination was reported at length in heavy, black-bordered columns.

The Lahaina-based whaling fleet was down to about a hundred vessels by 1865 when the long-rumored Confederate privateer appeared at Bonobe, Caroline Islands, and sank five ships. The privateer was a light combination sail and steam ship. She carried six guns. Her name was *Shenandoah*. Tradition has it that she was outfitted in New Zealand by a British group that sympathized with the Southern cause. Coaling stations were set up for her on various small Pacific Islands. Her master was a Captain Waddell.

Following the sinking of the five ships at Bonobe, the *Shenandoah* reappeared in June in the Arctic Ocean and set fire to 20 more Lahaina-based whalers. Five vessels were spared by Waddell to carry the crews, including several hundred Hawaiian sailors, to San Francisco. Although men on the whalers told the privateer captain the news about the surrender of Robert E. Lee, Waddell refused to believe that the Confederate cause was lost.

The war between the North and South cost the lives of half a million men. No other war in history was so bloody before or since. Nevertheless, the sacrifices demanded by war brought new maturity and stability to the United States.

As a nation, we became more determined to make "government of the people, by the people, for the people" work. We became more skilled in compromising and cooperating. We became more inclined to regard basic principles like the Four Freedoms as ideals toward which we must strive, rather than moral truths requiring "the last full measure of devotion."

Thus, by fire and blood the Civil War welded a diverse people into one indivisible nation. The stage was prepared for the modern world leadership of the United States.

Destiny was also at work in Hawaii. Sugar became King Sugar. The whalers vanished. Hereditary chiefs were replaced by elected monarchs. New oriental races came to throw in their lot with people already in the Islands.

As early as the reign of Kamehameha III, there was some agitation for annexation with the United States. Each succeeding king had to face more of the same. The Civil War provided a short respite from the pressure, but the very strength of the united country that emerged after the conflict exerted an irresistible magnetic influence.

Finally, Old Hawaii passed into legend. The crucial years that marked the division between the old and the new were those of the great American Civil War.

LAHAINA IS SHOWCASE OF OLD HAWAII

No town in all the Islands can rival Lahaina for historic symbols marking the steps of modern Hawaii's dramatic emergence from its colorful, pagan past. The main block of town alone provides sightseers with a fascinating excursion back through the years.

The block is famed because of Hawaii's largest banyan tree which stands near its center. But, there are many other things worth discovering nearby, all within easy walking distance of the massive, 85-year-old banyan.

Walk down Canal Street past Kam III School (where the royal palace was) to Wharf Street. A canal, now filled in, used to follow this course.

Often as many as 500 whaling ships at a time wintered in Lahaina Roads during the period from 1840 to 1865. Boats from the ship came up the canal to take on fresh water at the old Spring House which is at the back of Rainbow Inn. It was on one of these trips up the canal that a sailor emptied a can of old water and thus introduced the mosquito to Maui.

Beside the flagpole on Wharf Street are four rusted cannon. They were raised from the wreck of a Russian ship in Honolulu Harbor around 1816, and were brought to Lahaina to defend the capital. Ruins of the old fort are believed to be buried in the beach fronting the small boat harbor.

Across the street is the Lahaina Court House, built in 1857, just three years after the capital of Hawaii moved from Lahaina to Honolulu.

Down the way is Pioneer Hotel with its quaint Old Whalers Grog Shoppe. Patrons once tied their horses and buggies to the kiawe tree beside the road. Replete with rustic charm, the Shoppe was a natural setting for scenes of the Hollywood movie, **Twilight for the Gods,** which were filmed in Lahaina.

In front of the Shoppe are an old iron cauldron, once used on Kahoolawe, and an anchor, uncovered in the sand of Kaanapali.

Beyond this, just over the seawall at the end of the Lahaina Light & Power Co. is a sacred stone, the Hauola Stone. An old legend tells us that Hauola, a young girl, was turned to stone by the gods to save her from enemies. Kahunas often sent their patients to bathe in the sacred water there and many were reported cured.

Walking now up Market Street and back out to Front Street, you will come to the Maui Divers shop where interesting displays from the deep can be seen. The shop is run by renowned skin divers and has a special, uncommercialized atmosphere.

On the other side of the street is the missionary-style Baldwin House, now a community center.

Built in 1832, it was occupied by the Rev. D.D. Baldwin, M.D., and his family from 1836 to 1871. The house probably looked extremely foreign when first built in the midst of grass shacks and taro patches. It was the birthplace of one of the founders of HC&S, H.P. Baldwin.

WAILUKU TOUR RECREATES MISSIONARY DAYS

Imagine away the government buildings, the offices, all signs of modern life along High Street and Iao Road and you will have recreated the setting of the active missionary station that Wailuku was more than a century ago. For after the modern buildings have dropped to the background, landmarks of this active mission settlement remain to visit and enjoy today.

Most familiar perhaps is Kaahumanu Church, especially because of its bell which peals hourly. Incidentally, the clock which operates the bell is an eight-day clock, serviced and wound once a week.

The real name of the church is The Wailuku First Church. However, legend has it that Queen Kaahumanu visited Maui a year before her death in 1832, and seeing natives building a temporary church structure on the site asked them to name it after her.

The sign in front of the Church bears the date 1837. Nevertheless, the few records available indicate that in 1831 the Rev. J. S. Green broke ground for a church at Wailuku (obviously the one Queen Kaahumanu saw under construction) and that the present Kaahumanu Church with the New England influence obvious in its architecture, was started in 1839 under the Rev. Richard Armstrong.

The Rev. Armstrong was a noted builder of churches; he also started early sugar mills and saw mills. And, he built the home on the mission grounds on Iao Road, now the Wailuku Union parsonage. The entrance to the grounds is just above the small Kaahumanu cemetery. In this house, General Samuel C. Armstrong, founder of Hampton Institute (co-educational college for negroes in Virginia) was born in 1839.

Traditionally this was the parsonage for the missionaries in charge of the vast Wailuku congregation (once numbering 3700). It also was the home occupied by the Rev. and Mrs. William P. Alexander. Fondly known by Mauians as Father and Mother Alexander, William and Mary Alexander were parents of S. T. Alexander, partner of another well-known missionary son.

Also farther up Iao Road is the home of the Edward Bailey's built in 1841. This was the year the Rev. J. S. Green asked Mr. Bailey to succeed him as head of the Wailuku Female Seminary. The walls of the Bailey home are 20 inches thick, made of stone, and covered with plaster. The plaster was strengthened by mixing human hair, contributed by Hawaiian women.

One of the Alexanders' grandsons recalls running over to Mr. Bailey's sugar mill for molasses to have with his morning pancakes.

An enterprising man, Mr. Bailey operated both a sugar mill and a flour mill near his home. Both mills were run by mill wheels driven by a stream which passed through what was the yard of the Wailuku Sugar Co. manager's home. Part of the old aqueduct can be seen still.

The flour mill was a primitive affair but served its purpose. At one time Maui exported flour to California, and thousands of acres of wheat were growing at Makawao and Wailuku.

None of the buildings of the old seminary remain today except one which served as a kitchen-dining room. Standing behind the Bailey home, the building also served as a pay station for mill workers.

The historic Bailey Home became the Maui Historical Society museum, Hale Hoikeiki (House of Display), and was dedicated July 6, 1957, the 120th anniversary of the day the Wailuku Female Seminary opened.

EXPLORE ANCIENT RUINS AT LA PEROUSE

Jean Francois de Galaup, Comte de La Perouse (pronounced pay-rooz), famed French navigator, spent a single day, May 28, 1786, on Maui. Yet, the tiny double bay where his two ships anchored has been called La Perouse down to our own times.

According to his journal, the Comte came ashore and walked through several villages where he traded with the natives for 100 hogs, fresh vegetables, and several feather cloaks and helmets. After taking on fresh water, his ships sailed away. His journal survives only because he entrusted it to a passing ship. The fate of Comte de La Perouse, himself, is a mystery of the sea. It is believed that his ships were wrecked at Vanikoro Island in the Solomons, and survivors were devoured by cannibals.

Today, we can walk through the ruins of the villages seen by the French navigator. The streets are still there. Foundations of houses are still there. We can draw water from the ancient wells.

Just as the ruins of Pompeii show how life was in ancient Rome, the ruins of La Perouse show us something of the life of old Hawaii.

To get to La Perouse, one must drive over the narrow road beyond Makena. The road crosses a lava flow 600 years old, but which looks as fresh as many recent flows on the Big Island. The flow juts out to form one breakwater protecting the bay. Hardy souls (with stout shoes) may want to explore this flow. High up there are tree molds. Among the sea are interesting tide pools. Very prominent are three rocks—people turned to stone, according to a legend that parallels the Biblical story of Lot and his wife.

The road ends at a parking place near the ruins of a heiau. Stone walls still intact are about seven feet high and ten feet thick. Here the inner bay can be seen from a fence which circles a private residence. Actually, the inner bay is the remains of an old, man-made fish pond. It is entirely private property.

Starting at the heiau and going in the other direction, a well defined trail leads along the shore, through a gate, and across a second lava flow. This flow dates from around 1750 and is the most recent eruption of the Haleakala volcanic complex.

The trail is part of the King's Way which once circled Maui. It was built long before the days of Kamehameha the Great.

Once past the gate, a second trail branches makai from the King's Way. Here smooth beach stones have been laid on the rough lava.

This crude paving made the streets more visible at night, and made it possible for the barefooted villagers to get about town.

Along the stepping-stone-like streets are walled yards surrounding the stone foundations of long-gone grass houses. The floors are still covered with smooth sand or cinders. Here and there is a smooth stone which once served as a chair. Beside each house is a rubbish pile of shells.

Near the sea are two brackish wells. Like those of Egypt, they are cone-shaped. We can imagine the villagers walking down into them to fill their calabashes with water.

From the parking area to the ruins is a little over a mile. Numerous tree-shaded coves along the way make delightful picnicking or camping spots.

For those who enjoy the sport, La Perouse is also famous for its fishing.

Beyond everything else, out on the lava flows, it is easy to believe that Haleakala is just napping—that Pele could awaken at any moment to send angry rivers of molten rock again surging down to the sea.

STRANGE FOLK TALES HEARD AT WAIHEE

Thick as the mist in Waihee Valley is the veil separating modern Waihee from its past.

In the early days of the kingdom, Waihee was far more important than Wailuku, and it became a virtual boom town with the advent of sugar.

Today, it is just a quiet community, but much fun to visit. As you turn off harbor road to Waihee, look up at the sandhill with the water tower upon it. Here is one of the grandest heiaus in existence. Prisoners from Olinda restored the walls of the temple for the public to enjoy.

It was here that Kamehameha I offered thanksgiving after his victory in the battle of Kepaniwai in Iao in 1790.

Old timers say that everywhere you looked in Waihee there seemed to be a heiau, testifying to the importance and large population of the area.

Most of these are overgrown and forgotten. Thus, the Waihee area is highly recommended to anyone who likes to explore and discover lost vintages of the past for himself—secret caves, sacred stones, heiaus. Local talk gives clues, and a search is a wonderful group-outing plan.

Grandmothers of Waihee still recall the folk tales concerning mysterious events in the area which they learned as children. A favorite is about the phantom procession of spirits that came down from the hills to promenade through the village each month on the night of the god, Kane. Weird flute music accompanied the parade. Over the years many have heard it but none can capture the tune.

Another well-known tale is about the wahine mo'o (mermaids) that lived in Peeloko (secret pond) across from the Catholic cemetery. Due to the disappearance of nearby taro patches, it is dry today and full of bullrushes. The wahine mo'o were extremely beautiful women, and like the Sirens of the Odyssey, they lured men to destruction. The story is told of a merchant who was lured by the nymphs and later was discovered witless near Peeloko.

When Waihee was a thriving sugar area, there were theaters, saloons, coffee shops, and dance halls throughout the bustling town.

Samuel T. Alexander (partner in founding modern HC&S) and Parker Makee (son of Captain James Makee who owned Ulupalakua Ranch) started the plantation at Waihee.

KAHAKULOA'S SECRETS

On nearly every map of Maui, Kahakuloa is listed as a "Hawaiian Village." Although it no longer is a cluster of grass shacks, or a community of primitive people, the description is appropriate. Kahakuloa is a remote, more or less isolated, village occupied exclusively by Hawaiian people.

The road from Waihee to the village is not paved, but it is in fairly good condition. This road continues on past Kahakuloa toward Lahaina, and many people make an around-the-island jaunt of the trip. It is not recommended traveling on this road because of several dangerous spots.

After leaving Waihee for Kahakuloa, few landmarks can be seen except for a couple of ranch homes, sheer cliffs, rolling plains, and white, ribbon-like waterfalls dropping hundreds of feet down fern-grown slopes. And, of course, as you near Kahakuloa (the name Ka-haku-loa means the big bulge), there is the famed point, Maui's own Sugar Loaf.

The little village is situated at the mouth of Kahakuloa Valley. Fresh water fish, oopu, can be caught in the stream which comes down from the deep valley and passes through the village.

Many years ago most Kahakuloans lived in grass houses. Later, lumber was brought into the valley and the grass shacks started to disappear. Ships brought the bundles of lumber and dumped them into the ocean beyond the shallow bay. The people went out in their canoes to bring in the bundles.

Many legends are told about Kahakuloa. One is that a human, now turned into a huge, brown shark, has lived in the waters off Kahakuloa Point for generations.

The Hawaiians do not fish in this spot because chiefs have perished there by leaping off the famed cliff into the sea, and their royal blood still is mixed with the water. Some report that the cliff sways back and forth to frighten away fishermen.

There are, of course, many other excellent fishing spots, for both surf casting and spear fishing, around Kahakuloa which are not taboo.

OCTAGON CHURCH MAY REPRESENT CROWN

One of the unique sights of the Valley Isle is the eight-sided Holy Ghost Catholic Church in Kula. Its white walls and gleaming metal roof can be seen for miles around. Its door is never locked.

Today, not even the members of the active parish know for certain why the church was built as an octagon. However, there is reason to believe that it was designed to resemble the eight-sided, silver crown displayed in the church.

Traditionally the crown symbol is linked to Roman churches of the Holy Ghost with Portuguese congregations because of a thanksgiving offering made by a queen of Portugal who lived in the Fourteenth Century.

Queen Elizabeth, known as the Holy Queen, prayed to the Holy Ghost to deliver her drought-stricken country from famine. When rain came, she gave her crown to the church.

Father James designed and built the Kula church. Construction started in 1894 and the church was finished two years later.

There have been several attempts to explain why the church is octagonal. A once-popular story was that Russian immigrants built the church to resemble churches in their homeland.

Another is that many churches of the plains of Portugal are eight-sided to withstand winds.

The first Mass of the Holy Ghost Church was celebrated in 1895 although construction had not been entirely completed.

In 1897, the alter arrived from Austria. This elaborate replica of a Gothic cathedral is embellished with fine detail work, religious paintings in rich color, and statuary.

The altar and the 14 Stations of the Cross hung in the church were done by the same craftsman.

The silver crown in the Kula Holy Ghost Church arrived from the Azores in 1891. Funds to buy it came from house-to-house solicitation.

When the crown arrived on Maui, an old Portuguese custom was followed. On Easter Sunday, 50 days before the feast honoring the Holy Ghost (Pentecost), a drawing was held. Those who drew tickets numbered one through seven were allowed to keep the crown in their homes.

The family holding ticket number seven kept the crown from Holy Ghost day until Easter of the following year.

In 1896, when the church was completed, the crown was housed in it permanently.

Now, only on Holy Ghost Sunday is it removed. After Mass, it is taken from the church, followed by a procession, to the nearby church hall.

Celebration of Holy Ghost Sunday is a big event for the Kula parish. A huge luau is staged and the public is invited to attend the festivities of Maui's unusual eight-sided church.

VISITING HANA—VAST TROPICAL PLAYGROUND

Perhaps the loveliest, most charming area on the Valley Isle is Hana—birthplace of alii, land of caves, jungles, pools, and waterfalls.

The drive over takes about two hours and much of the road is not good. However, there are excellent rest parks along the way to allow visitors to enjoy the scenery at their leisure. The first, reached after about an hour on the road, is Kaumahina. It is equipped with restrooms, woodsy looking tables and benches, barbecue pits, and shelters. From this park, you can look out across a turquoise sea upon Keanae peninsula, where a Hawaiian village, complete with an old stone church and taro patches, is situated.

After another 30 minutes on the road, you will come to Puu Kaa Park. This is much smaller than Kaumahina, but it has its own special attraction—a natural swimming pool refreshed constantly by a mountain stream.

After this, Hana is the next stop. As you enter the residential district, be on the lookout for the marker which points out the road to Maui's Blue Grotto, Wainapanapa Caves.

Wainapanapa (meaning sparkling water) is a double cave. The lower part, whose entrance we see filled with mirror-like water, is part of a lava tube. The water, when viewed from inside sparkles with beautiful blue lights. The dry, hidden upper cave was formed by the dislodgement of loose clinker. To enter the upper room, people (equipped with waterproof flashlights) dive under the jutting ledge beyond which the cavern opens into a low-roofed chamber. It was here that the princess Popoalae hid, fearing the jealousy of her husband, Kakae.

One day while searching for his wife near Wainapanapa, Kakae saw a strange shadow in the water of Wainapanapa. Watching it, he discovered that it was the reflection of a kahili which was being waved by Popoalae's handmaid. Kakae knew instantly that his wife was within.

With his men, he swam into the cave and slew the two women. To this day it is said that the walls and roof of the cave are covered with the life blood of Popoalae.

Just one of the many other points of interest in Hana is Kauiki, the famed fortress hill overlooking Puekahi Bay. At the west side of Kauiki, you may see the tiny cave in which Queen Kaahumanu was born.

Moaning waters can be heard in Hana. Follow the road leading out of town in the direction of Hamoa Beach and turn off at the sign marking Kuula's Sacred Fish Pond. On the beach you will see the lava-covered eel-monster which it is said, was dragged ashore and killed for stealing fish from the pond. The nearby rocks form the petrified watch dog put there to guard the body. The squeals and moans of the ocean are the cries of friends come to mourn the eel who was actually a demi-god.

Eastward is Ka Iwi o Pele hill, where tradition says one of Pele's mortal bodies is buried.

You have heard the legend of the woman who leaped up to the moon. It was from one of these hills, Kauiki or Ka Iwi o Pele, that she was supposed to have jumped. No great feat this really, for ancient Hawaiians believed that over this area, heaven bent closet to earth. Perhaps it is so—and thus to this day, beautiful Hana is called heavenly.

DWIGHT BALDWIN
Letter of Recommendation

When Dwight Baldwin the missionary patriarch was on the brink of embarking upon his chosen mission, he handed the following letter of recommendation to Charlotte Fowler, the woman he wanted to share with him his life's work:

August 14, 1830

Dear Madame,

The person who will hand this letter to you is Mr. Dwight Baldwin, a dear friend of mine, and who, from several years of intimate acquaintance, has obtained the highest place in my confidence.

Mr. Baldwin, as you know is going abroad as a missionary of the crop. For this employment I think him to be fitly qualified, on account of his ardent piety, decision of character, fortitude and patience, and literary and theological attainments.

Mr. Baldwin, as well as all who are friendly to the mission in which he is engaged, thinks it proper that he should take with him a companion who shall share with him in all the pleasures, honours and precious toils of a missionary life.

Should Mr. Baldwin think proper to make any proposals to you Madam to become his bosom companion, and to show this letter to you, this will inform you of my opinion concerning his character, and also concerning the kind of husband you will find in him should you feel disposed to accept of his proposition. Besides, what I have said concerning his character, I would add that the temper of Mr. B. is mild, uniform and peculiarly kind and affectionate - In his intercourse with all he is frank, open, and honest. Free from all the acts of management and worldly policy, he expresses what he means simply, with a view to be understood and being strictly conscientious and honest, full confidence may be placed in what he says.

I write this, my dear friend, as a friend of mission and as a friend to domestic peace and happiness. Should you feel willing to engage in a missionary life and be pleased with the personal appearance of Mr. Baldwin, it is my honest conviction that you will find in him, a kind, indulgent, sympathizing and truly affectionate husband, and of course, that you need not be fearful and backward in encouraging his approaches.

You may think it desirable to learn something farther respecting Mr. Baldwin. This information you may, perhaps, receive from Messrs. Tinker and Dibble, in the most satisfactory manner, as they have been acquainted with him for years, and they expect to be engaged with him in the same mission.

I hope a gracious Lord will guide you both in such a way as will be best for his glory and your good.

I am your friend

M. L. R. PERRINE

The missionary doctor Dwight Baldwin and his wife arrived at Lahaina in 1835, after serving for four years as a doctor at the medical rest station at Waimea on the Big Island. Rev. Baldwin welcomed the assignment to Lahaina, thinking he would be able to devote himself fully to missionary work but he soon learned that he was the only missionary on Maui, Molokai and Lanai qualified to practice medicine.

Baldwin Home was built in 1834 with thick walls of coral and stone, and hand-hewn timbers. The Baldwins moved into the original section in 1838 and in 1840 added a bedroom and study. In 1849, the Rev. Baldwin added a complete second story to house the addition of six Baldwin children. Baldwin Home did not suffer for any lack of visitors in those days. There were visits by other missionary families, government officials and captains of the whaling ships that put into Lahaina.

Whale oil was used to light the lamps and a barrel would last for a year. Flour was brought around the Horn by the missionary steamer Morning Star and had been wetted so much that the daily measure for cooking had to be chiseled off. The family had their own vegetable garden and there was no lack of fruit from the guava, mango and bananas.

EMILY ALEXANDER BALDWIN

Upon the death of his mother in 1943, Arthur D. Baldwin wrote and published the following tribute to her:

Emily Whitney Alexander, later Mrs. Henry P. Baldwin, lived for nearly all of her life on the Island of Maui. She was born on January 18, 1846 at Lahainaluna, Maui, where her father, the missionary William P. Alexander, was head of the school for Hawaiian boys. There she spent her early childhood. Her playmates were her brothers and sisters and the children of Father and Mother Baldwin who lived in Lahaina, one of whom was Emily's future husband Henry P. Baldwin.

When she was nine years old, in 1855, Father Alexander, became of failing health and seeking an outdoor life, gave up his position at Lahaina and for a few months moved his family to Ulupalakua where he managed the Torbert cattle ranch. This was just prior to the purchase of the Ulupalakua property by Captain Makee. Mrs. Baldwin often told of her recollections of the Ulupalakua of that time,—of the fun she had with Wilhelmina Makee, later Mrs. Spalding, of moaning cattle dying of the drought, of expeditions on horseback to neighboring villages with her father, who preached to Hawaiian congregations summoned by the blowing of conch shells. She remembered well the heavy forests in Ulupalakua and Kula, the only remnant of which is now the dying forest of Kanaio.

After leaving Ulupalakua the Alexander family moved to the old home still standing in Wailuku. Here Father Alexander took up the pastorate of Hawaiian churches in Wailuku, Waihee and Waikapu. He used to ride from one church to the other, often taking Emily with him. They were a most intimate father and daughter.

The children's early schooling was given them by their father. Later, they were sent to Punahou, with intervals at home when the money for the schooling was lacking.

Following her graduation Emily taught mathematics and other subjects in Punahou, her pupils including Samuel Parker, Samuel Wilcox, Frank Damon, William O. Smith, W. R. Castle and Charles M. Cooke, most of whom were only two or three years her junior.

Then shortly after the Civil War she made a visit to the "States." She was insufficiently financed for the trip by her earnings and a little money given her by her father. On the trip she was often embarrassed by her homemade dresses but had no money with which to buy fashionable clothes.

She stayed first with her brother James who was then a pastor in San Leandro, California. During the visit James was married to Mary Webster "Aunt Mary James" for whom Emily was a bridesmaid.

After James' wedding she went for a trip to the "States" traveling alone by steamer to the Isthmus of Panama, across it by rail and then to New York by steamer. For a young girl from the Hawaii of those days it was a long and difficult trip which showed her courage and ability to look after herself.

In New York and the Middle West and South she visited Alexander relatives, including the Graydons and Alexanders of Indianapolis, the Samuel and John Alexanders of Southern Indiana, the Martins of Evansville, Indiana and her Aunt Anne Gass and daughters at Gallatin, Tennessee. Some of these relatives, particularly Cousin Hay Gass (Harris) and the Alexander and Graydons of Indianapolis and the Martins, became her lifelong friends. She never made mistakes in her intimate friendships and they were always for life.

After these visits she was bridesmaid at her sister Annie's marriage to Chas. H. Dickey in Whitehall, Illinois. They were the much loved Uncle and Aunt whom the Baldwin children so well remember at Haiku.

With the Dickeys Emily spent a happy year at Whitehall and then sailed back to the Islands, as she had come, via Panama and San Francisco. On Maui she returned to the Wailuku parsonage with her father and mother. At this time Henry Baldwin was a luna on Waihee Plantation. One day Emily rode with him in Iao Valley, a momentous ride from which they returned affianced husband and wife. They were married by Father Alexander in the church in Wailuku on April 5, 1870.

Following his marriage Mr. Baldwin in partnership with his brother-in-law Samuel T. Alexander under the name of Alexander and Baldwin started the original sugar plantation at Paia, which, with drought (there was no irrigation) and low prices to contend with, had for some time very hard going. During this period Emily kept the plantation books and often wrote business letters for her husband.

For twelve years the family lived at Sunnyside where the six older children were born. Then after a year in San Francisco they moved to the old home at Haiku.

There were intervals when the family lived at Makaweli, Kauai in 1893 and in Spreckelsville in the early 1900s and then the last move was made to the home at Maluhia, Makawao, where Mr. and Mrs. Baldwin spent the rest of their lives.

By this time the children had grown up and had their own establishments and many grandchildren and great-grandchildren came into being.

After her husband's death Mrs. Baldwin, as she had during his lifetime, attended almost without fail the weekly services at the Henry P. Baldwin Memorial church at Paliuli, after which followed the never to be forgotten Sunday dinners at Maluhia. It was the time for the gathering of the family, young and old.

The dinner was usually attended by some of the sons and daughters, but in the afternoon grandchildren and great-grandchildren also would come in. All of these gatherings centered, of course, about Mrs. Baldwin, who greatly enjoyed the conversation and fun, in which she often took part with the delightful humor for which her father is still remembered.

Then in the early morning of August 30, 1942 she fell, breaking her hip, and never walked again. Mercifully her memory had failed to a considerable degree and she would forget that she was and had been ill for so long. Always during her illness she recognized her children and spoke lovingly of and to them.

Appendix

LIFE AND CHARACTER OF HENRY PERRINE BALDWIN

In 1915, Arthur D. Baldwin, son of Henry Perrine Baldwin, wrote a beautiful and interesting memorial to his father—A MEMOIR OF HENRY PERRINE BALDWIN—which was published in a limited edition for private distribution by the family. The following extract from this publication personifies an innermost expression of respect, love and affection:

A MEMOIR OF
Henry Perrine Baldwin
1842 TO 1911

BY

ARTHUR D. BALDWIN

His life was gentle; and the elements
So mix'd in him that Nature might stand up,
And say to all the world, This was a man!

PRIVATELY PRINTED AT CLEVELAND
January the second
MCMXV

H. P. Baldwin

Life and Character of Henry Perrine Baldwin

DWIGHT BALDWIN, father of Henry Perrine Baldwin, was born at Durham, Connecticut, in 1798, but with his parents made his home after 1804 at Durham, New York. The first two years of his college course were taken at Williams, but later, after an interval of teaching school, he graduated from Yale in 1821, and subsequently began the study of medicine while at the same time teaching a school in Durham, New York. What followed is thus stated in the Baldwin Genealogy written by his friend and relative, Charles C. Baldwin of Cleveland:

> The three years allowed for studying a profession had not elapsed, when he met with a change in his religious views. His mind had been awakened to the interests of the soul when he was a member of Yale College. Those impressions had not entirely worn off, but now, under the faithful preaching of their pastor, Rev. Dr. Williston, his attention was called up to the subject of religion as it had never been before. About the first of March, 1826, he found relief in believing in an Almighty Redeemer, a hope which has never forsaken him. Religion became the all-absorbing subject of his thought by day and by night. His pious friends now urged him to leave the profession which he had chosen, and direct his attention to the Christian ministry, and some suggested that his knowledge of medicine would not be needed at home, but would increase his usefulness in some benighted land. He soon came to the same conclusion himself, and September 3rd of that year, he united with the Congrega-

Dwight and Charlotte Fowler Baldwin

tional Church in Durham, New York, and soon after he entered the Theological Seminary at Auburn, where he spent three years. While at Auburn he offered his services to the American Board of Boston for a Foreign Mission, and they were accepted. Therefore, when his course at Auburn was completed, they sent for him to go to Boston to attend the Medical Lectures at Cambridge, that he might in that department be better prepared for the missionary service.

Having come to this momentous decision, it was evidently of the greatest importance that he should have a wife to share in his labors, and accordingly he was introduced by a friend to Charlotte Fowler, daughter of Deacon Solomon Fowler of North Branford, Connecticut, and a few weeks later was married to her on December 3, 1830. Twenty-five days later they set sail with a company of missionaries on the ship New England on the long trip around Cape Horn, destined for the Sandwich Islands as the Hawaiian group was then called. This, the "fourth reinforcement," on June 21, 1831 arrived at Honolulu, where they received an enthusiastic welcome from the half naked Hawaiians who plunged joyously into the surf to carry the new missionaries ashore.

Years afterward, when Mrs. Baldwin for the first time revisited her friends and family in New England, she told them that not once on that long, stormy, hard trip around the cape, nor yet once in the years of ministry that followed, had she regretted that apparently hasty resolution to marry the young missionary and depart with him, leaving behind so much that was dear, for a new and almost unknown world.

Stationed first at Waimea, Hawaii, Dwight Baldwin's health suffered in the rigorous climate of that place and they moved to Lahaina on the Island of Maui.

Lahaina was one of the principal homes of the Hawaiian kings, and was, and is, a very lovely place, with its luxuriant tropical growth, its foreground of sea and its background of precipitous forest covered mountains. It was a thriving harbor in those days, being a port of call for the whale ships which sometimes filled the bay so full that one could jump from one deck to another. Here for thirty-four years Dwight Baldwin did his great life work, preaching to the native congregations in the old Wainee church, and serving as government physician for the Islands of Maui, Molokai, and Lanai.

In 1868 Father Baldwin (so the early missionaries were known) resigned his Lahaina pastorate and became associated with Reverend B. W. Parker in the conduct of the native Theological Seminary at Honolulu. Mother Baldwin died in 1873. She is described as exceptionally sweet, of quiet dignity, and well beloved by her family and friends. Her husband followed her in 1886. As the inscription on her tombstone reads, it had been for both "A life of work, love and prayer," a life intensely and sincerely religious, full of the stern old New England sort of virtue, yet withal exceedingly kindly, unselfish, and affectionate.

Henry Perrine Baldwin was the sixth of eight children and was born August 29, 1842 in the old Baldwin homestead (now the Baldwin House Social Settlement) at Lahaina.

In this old house built of coral rock and plaster, and situated a few rods from the sea in a setting of

The Old Baldwin Home at Lahaina, Maui

Now known as "Baldwin House," a Social Settlement

guava, mango, and breadfruit trees, live what memories of the old missionary days! In fact in an old box in the attic for many years the curious might have found a quantity of correspondence between the missionary fathers, which told the story of the unceasing battle that was fought with heathen customs and renegade whites, the fight for the establishment of virtue and the expulsion of vice from the land. The missionaries took their troubles to God with the most perfect faith and received their answer, and these letters sound as if to all intents they *talked* with Him face to face.

In the midst of such influences Henry Baldwin grew up in the old Baldwin home. Here he shared with his brother Charles the long room in the second story. A room in the north wing of the house was used by Father Baldwin as his dispensary and schoolroom for his children. No other teaching than his own was available, but no doubt the children did not suffer on that account.

Their schooling included also a strict religious education. Every morning and evening "prayers" were held, which consisted in a reading from the Bible, the singing of hymns and a prayer by Father Baldwin, or some distinguished guest who might be present. Henry Baldwin, who had a natural aptitude for music, while still very young used to lead the hymns on the melodeon at morning and evening prayer.

On this same instrument at so early an age as seven, he played the hymns at the Seamen's Chapel where services were held in English by Dr. Sereno E.

Bishop. Father Baldwin used to preach in Hawaiian at the old Wainee church at the south end of town where native Hawaiian congregations assembled often numbering as many as a thousand souls. Of the membership of this church were John Ii and Timateo, who at one time joined the old order with the new by saluting each other according to the ancient custom, touching noses in the midst of the service.

The great feature of the religious and social life was the "General Meeting" which was held annually at Honolulu. The party from Lahaina consisted, among others, of the Baldwin, Alexander, Bishop, Taylor, and Forbes families. Sturdy Kanakas would carry the missionaries and their children one by one through the water to row boats which conveyed them to the waiting sailing vessel, there to proceed upon their slow and odorous course to Honolulu (not until 1853 when the little Akamai appeared, were there any steam driven craft in those waters). The travellers carried their own food and bedding, laying the latter on deck. Sometimes as many as five dreadful days would pass before the weary voyagers arrived at their destination. In Honolulu the Baldwins used to stay with the Cookes at the Pioneer Mission, whither they rode on horseback, while their baggage was carried by hand carts or oxcarts, for horse carriages did not exist in Honolulu during the early days of the mission. Then, while their elders attended the missionary meetings, the youngsters enjoyed glorious good times.

At Lahaina the children had in the sea the greatest

101

Approaching the Town of Lahaina
on the Island of Maui

of all playgrounds. Taught by old Kealoha, their nurse, they all learned to swim like natives. Henry Baldwin used in fact to say, when still a very small child, that he believed he could swim best at the bottom. The Lahaina natives were famous swimmers and many were the tales he used to tell in later life of their skill in spearing fish while swimming under water, of exploits with sharks, and of other swimming feats often performed by the old natives, but quite unknown in these degenerate days. With such teachers it is not surprising that the Baldwin boys became expert with the canoe and in the water.

They were not allowed, however, according to the general understanding among the missionaries, to become too intimate with the native Hawaiians, because of their different standard of morality. The use of the native language accordingly (as recommended by the "General Meeting") was tabued until the boys were twelve years old. But for this prohibition no doubt Henry Baldwin would have been, when he grew to manhood, a more proficient scholar in the Hawaiian language. Nevertheless he was able to use it fluently and well, though not sufficiently so to satisfy himself.

The most intimate friends of the family on Maui were the Alexanders, who lived nearby at Lahaina-luna, where Father Alexander taught the school until in 1857, to the great regret of the Baldwins, he moved to Wailuku on the other side of the West Maui Mountains. With the Alexanders often the merriest expeditions used to be undertaken to the woods and mountains. One of their favorite picnic spots was

Henry Perrine Baldwin

In early Youth

Halealoha in beautiful Koulu Valley, a little house built by the natives for Mother Baldwin's use when recovering from a long period of sickness.

On all such expeditions, as on the trips to General Meeting at Honolulu, Henry Baldwin was said to be "the life of the party." We hear of his riding his horse, "Jolly," into the dining-room to frighten his sisters, and we also hear that they always came to him when in trouble. Full of energy in fun as in work, he was always active. At the same time he was exceedingly conscientious. It is told how at one time a picnic in one of the mountain valleys was planned, and Henry was urged to join the party, but declined, much as he loved such expeditions, because of unfinished work in the garden. He always believed that what he set his hands to do must be well finished before undertaking other things. In many such ways the child was father to the man. Kind, cheerful, and capable, he was depended upon by others, and, making many friends and holding them fast, he was from the beginning a natural leader through that rare combination of fun, sympathy, and conscience, for which he was well known in after life.

It was a very simple, healthy life, that of the early Hawaiian missionaries. Father Baldwin's salary was only six hundred dollars a year which, however, was eked out with a small income possessed by Mother Baldwin. On this was supported a family of six children (two had died) besides which many friends were entertained. Missionaries often visited them and many captains of whalers spent their time on shore with the family, sometimes leaving their wives while they themselves went on their way to northern waters. On one such occasion a captain sailed away leaving his wife behind but neither he nor his ship was ever heard from again.

A barrel of whale oil furnished light for a year. The flour brought by the missionary steamer Morning Star came once a year and several times it had been so wetted in the storms off Cape Horn that it had hardened and it was necessary to chisel off the daily measure for cooking. Vegetables, however, grew in their own garden and there was an abundance of fruit, such as bananas, grapes, and watermelons, and one does not hear that they suffered from their poverty.

In 1856 the health of Father Baldwin, who had worked thirty-six years without a vacation, failed and the "American Board" granted him a year's leave of absence. Accompanied by his wife he left the Islands for a year's visit in "the states," sailing on the bark Behring Sea by way of Cape Horn. After a happy reunion with his daughter, Abigail, a Mount Holyoke girl, and his son Dwight, a student at Yale College, and with his old friends and kindred, he returned to the Islands with his wife and daughter by way of the Isthmus of Panama, improved in health though in place of rest he had spent much of his time preaching in various pulpits.

While the parents and older children were in the United States, the boys Charles and Henry began their career at the boarding school at Punahou near Honolulu, then under the charge of Dr. Edward Beckwith. For him Henry Baldwin formed immediately a very great affection, which continued until this good man's death in 1909.

With him the boys spent some hard as well as pleasant days. Of the former kind were those during vacation time, when the boys were set by Mr. Spooner, the business manager of the school, to do man's work in the dairy and the field.

The great trial of the new scholars in those days, as for many years after, was the ceremony of "ducking" in the pond. It was a tradition that every new boy must be ducked, but Henry Baldwin, who began early to practice boxing with Samuel Alexander, Samuel Armstrong (afterwards General Armstrong of Hampton Institute) and others, put his back to the wall and invited the big boys of the school to "come on." He was not ducked.

His favorite recreation while at Punahou was to search the Oahu Mountains and valleys for land shells and ferns to add to his collection. On nearly every Saturday and holiday the boys would be off to the woods. Sometimes they scaled apparently impossible precipices. Often night would catch them still among the crags where, wet and hungry, they would make what shift they could until morning, returning then to mild scoldings by good Dr. Beckwith.

Immediately after completing his course at Punahou, Mr. Baldwin began his life as a planter by undertaking to manage William D. Alexander's rice plantation near the school. This was a complete failure, and thereafter his business activities were confined to the raising of sugar, in which, as will appear, he was more successful.

Emily Whitney Alexander

A Schoolgirl at Punahou

In 1863, when twenty-one years old, he began to work for his brother Dwight, who was planting sugar-cane at Lahaina and selling his product to Messrs. Campbell and Turton. It was his intention to earn enough money to finance the completion of his education at Williams College, and afterwards to take a course in a medical college. This ambition was never gratified, for once started at work, he stayed at it as long as he lived. Nevertheless he always keenly regretted his lack of a college education, notwithstanding that, possessed of an alert mind and a keen observation and helped by an extensive course of reading, he acquired a greater store of knowledge and culture than that of the majority of college men.

Not long after beginning work at Lahaina, he was persuaded by Samuel Alexander, manager of the Waihee plantation on the northeast side of the West Maui Mountains to take a position under him as head luna.

Many were the thrilling tales which he afterwards used to tell of those old days at Waihee. Among its laborers was a part of the first importation of Chinese to the Islands, which, as usually happened with the successive immigrations of various nationalities, turned out to be the worst. They were in fact a band of pirates and cutthroats, and it required a man of steady nerve and courage to hold his own among them. Mr. Baldwin alone among the lunas carried no weapons, and it was perhaps due to this fact and his ready courage and his ability to sympathize and "get on" with the working people, that he came through the ordeal unscathed. He did, however, carry a scar left by a stone thrown while quelling one of their riots.

The arguments of Christopher H. Lewers, owner of Waihee, had much to do with Mr. Baldwin's decision to abandon his plan of going to the states to study medicine. The young man was too promising and too much needed by the plantation to be readily given up. One can not but think at this day how great a difference it might have made with the Island of Maui if Mr. Baldwin, who was more responsible than any other for the making of its barren and almost desert districts into a prosperous, fruitful, and well inhabited country, had followed his inclination and become a physician instead of a business man!

In 1867 for the first time, he left the Islands to see something of the world, accompanied by his friend, Rexford Hitchcock. A diary kept of this trip is still preserved. It tells of an excursion to the Dalles of the Columbia, and a very difficult expedition to the Calaveras big trees, accomplished on foot through the deep snow and mountain torrents after stage and saddle horses failed. One finds manifested in this diary many of the characteristics which we associate with his later life, such as his intense love of travel and of mountain scenery, his love for music, and his sincere devotion to religion.

While in California on this trip he met his early friend and schoolmate, Miss Emily Whitney Alexander, who was in the States, visiting her brother James Alexander at San Leandro, California, and later her aunts Jane Graydon in Indianapolis and

Iao Valley

Maui, Hawaiian Islands

Anne Gass in Gallatin, Tennessee, and other relatives in different places.

Later, upon his return to the Islands, they became engaged to marry, the betrothal taking place in the beautiful Valley of Iao. The wedding was solemnized at Wailuku on April 5, 1870. Their first home was at Sunnyside (now the parsonage of the Makawao Foreign Protestant Church), where in the neighboring district of Paia, Mr. Samuel Alexander and Mr. Baldwin under the name of Alexander and Baldwin, had started a sugar plantation. From that time, Central Maui was Mr. Baldwin's home and the place of his principal activities.

Hard work and worry were his lot during those first years at Sunnyside. He was obliged to borrow in Honolulu the money (about nine hundred dollars) which it was necessary for him to contribute to the partnership, Mr. Alexander giving the larger share. Even so small a debt as this was then a very serious matter. The plantation was not irrigated and put all its dependence upon the chance of rain. Desolating droughts followed. With a small mill of a daily capacity of only three tons (its present capacity is two hundred tons) and with many adverse natural conditions, it is no wonder that the future sometimes looked to the young partners very dark indeed. It is told that at one time Mr. Baldwin in despair dismounted from his horse and prayed, promising that if God would send the rain which would save the plantation, he would thenceforth give a part of all he earned to His purposes. That very night

112

came the rain, sealing the covenant which was always scrupulously kept.

On October 5th, 1874, Father Baldwin wrote to him:

> You seem to keep up good courage about the plantation, but I think if you have one or two poor years your agents will own the whole. I have been easy about what you owe me. But as far as you find it convenient to pay up, it may enable me to help you the more hereafter should worse times come.

Mr. Baldwin worked very hard and indeed must have earned his salary of one hundred dollars a month, for at one and the same time he was manager, sugar-boiler, engineer, and bookkeeper. Mrs. Baldwin used often to help him with the bookkeeping in the evenings when he was too exhausted to "figure" after his heavy work all day in the fields.

Often it was hard for the family to make ends meet. Nevertheless there existed a spirit of hospitality in those days that poverty could not suppress, a spirit sometimes mistaken for extravagance. And so it happened that upon the visit of an old missionary friend to Sunnyside, for whom chickens were killed and the best that could be had provided, the young couple was taken sharply to task by their guest for their lavish living.

With the enactment of the first reciprocity treaty with the United States in 1876 the anxious partners were cheered by new hope. Mr. Baldwin's letters at this time were full of the negotiations which led up to the passage of this treaty, showing that even then he was consulted by the leaders and was active in public affairs.

Life and Character

On March 8, 1875, his father wrote him:

Rain, health, reciprocity and God's blessing will get you out of debt.

And so they did—with the help of the Hamakua ditch.

Before the better times came, however, and while this ditch project was under discussion, Mr. Baldwin met with an accident which nearly cost him his life. This occurred on March 28, 1876. Let me here quote Mr. W. H. Wilkinson who was engineer of the mill at that time:

The day the accident happened he was standing there throwing the cane back a long while. We were going to boil off that day. He came into the mill and said to me, "We have got to set that mill up more, there is too much waste." One side ground fairly well but the other side was a little more open so it did not crush the cane properly. I said, "Mr. Baldwin, we haven't got iron of the right thickness. If we put a sheet on this side it will be closer than the other side." He said, "Well, I will go up to dinner and when I come back we will take a look at it. Have the boys clean up the mill." At the time we were clearing up the ground of the last pieces of cane as it was the last of the day's run. This was just before the noon hour. He rode away and I told the boys to go to dinner but kept the boys that fed the mill to clean it up. I went out and helped them. We poured cream of lime on the rollers so as to keep them sweet. This when it dried was like whitewash. I went out and was looking at the rollers and being white I could see that they were nearly the same at both ends and I satisfied myself that we didn't have proper iron to set them up even.

Mr. Baldwin came up behind me on his horse and said, "Well, what do you think of it?" I said, "Well, Mr. Baldwin, I think just as I told you. We haven't any iron thin enough to make it even." He and I were the only ones there.

114

𝕰mily 𝕬lexander 𝕭aldwin   𝕳enry 𝕻errine 𝕭aldwin
In 1882   *In 1867*

115

Charlie Baldwin was down at the boilers. Mr. Baldwin repeated, "That is wider than you think for on that side." Then he rode off to hitch his horse and walked back up. While he was hitching his horse I walked around to the other side of the mill between it and the house. That was the side that was widest open.

Mr. Baldwin came up and stepped up on the plank where the man stood when he fed the mill. He was whittling a piece of shingle with which he was evidently going to prove his point, but he dropped it, changing his mind, and showed me by slipping his fingers in between the rollers where it was widest. It just touched the knuckles. The mill was going pretty fast. He reached over and slipped his hand in the place where the rollers were closest together. The rollers (which weighed about three tons) caught his finger and I knew that a pair of cattle could not pull him out and I ran into the door of the engine room which was some feet mauka of the rollers and around the engine intending to throw it out of gear.

In this moment of dreadful peril Mr. Baldwin retained his presence of mind. He called to Mr. Wilkinson to reverse the engine at once. To do this with the old fashioned engine (which may still be seen in the mud press of the Paia mill) it was necessary to push up the eccentric rod, insert a pin in the hole in the crank, and start the engine the opposite way. This complicated process Mr. Wilkinson was able to accomplish only just in time to save Mr. Baldwin's life. His narrative proceeds:

As soon as I got it stopped I had full control of it and I backed very slowly until I thought he was out, and I called out to him, "Are you all right?" He did not answer. I repeated the question several times but got no answer. If I had connected her she would have gone ahead and I couldn't disconnect her, so I called to Charlie to shut off the steam.

He saw something was wrong and went and shut off. Then I connected the engine and went out to see how Mr. Baldwin was and met him walking into the engine house. He was as white as a sheet. I set a chair for him to sit down and he reached around with his other hand and got out his keys and told me to send a man up to the office at Sunnyside and get a bottle of brandy. I told him I had some at my house and I went up and got it, my wife returning with me. I gave him some. I was very much afraid he would faint but he did not. He was in his shirt sleeves. The mill had stripped all the flesh from his hand and his arm to some distance above the elbow. The arteries were not severed and there was very little bleeding. After he had sat a while my wife and I supported him and got him over to my house which was just across the road, and he lay down on the bed.

I went back to the mill and wrote a letter to Drs. Enders or Moffatt or both, and sent a man with it to Wailuku (ten miles away). I explained in my note that they should come prepared to take the arm off. I put a bullock driver on Mr. Baldwin's horse and told him to ride as fast as he could, but to come back slowly. He did not obey me but went fast both ways and so injured the horse that he died soon after. The man spurred the horse and made him crazy so that he did not get to Wailuku as soon as he would otherwise. Dr. Moffatt saw him coming and feared something was wrong and met him at the gate and his horse being ready there was no more delay. He came up very quickly, and that afternoon performed the operation (amputation of the arm between the elbow and the shoulder).

As soon as the man was started for the doctor I wrote to Mr. S. T. Alexander at Haiku. He came over at once and brought Mrs. Dickey to stay with Mrs. Baldwin.

This occurred about a week before the birth of the author of this memoir. Under such circumstances, Mrs. Dickey hesitated to tell Mrs. Baldwin of the accident, but the latter, suspecting some untoward event, drew from her late in the evening an account of what had happened. Early next morning, she mounted a horse and rode down to her husband's bedside at Paliuli, a half mile away. Later, when Father and Mother Alexander arrived, she was taken in their buggy daily back and forth between Sunnyside and Paliuli, while Messrs. Samuel and Henry Alexander and Charles Dickey took turns with Mr. Baldwin at night.

In about two weeks' time he was sufficiently strong to return to Sunnyside. Almost immediately he began to readjust his plan of life to the loss of his arm. He practised writing with his left hand. He planned a cabinet organ with a pedal bass, and ordered one both for his own use and for the Church at Makawao, where he had been accustomed to play hymns for the services conducted by Father Green. This duty he continued to perform with his one hand for many years thereafter, and so faithful was he in its performance that on at least two very rainy occasions the preacher and his organist constituted the entire congregation. Nevertheless Father Green went through the service precisely as though the usual company had been present.

As early as the sixteenth of April, that is, less than three weeks after the accident, his sister, Mrs. S. M. Damon, wrote of having received a letter from him a day or two before, which must thus have been written within two weeks of the accident. Five weeks later, on the twenty-third of May, his sister, Mrs. Atwater, wrote that he must not write so many letters. She mentioned also that she was glad that Mrs. Baldwin and the baby were going up to Samuel Alexander's mountain house, Olinda, which must have been very recently built.

Letters received that spring, and some of them still preserved, evidence the affection and respect which Mr. Baldwin had already won for himself throughout the group. Among others Sanford B. Dole, afterwards president of the Hawaiian Republic and first governor of the Territory, wrote, addressing him as "Dear old Friend:"

> Your conduct at the time of the accident and afterwards seems to me wonderfully brave and heroic and I congratulate you on it. Such a spirit, I am sure robs the affairs of much of its suffering, both with yourself and your friends.

On April 26, 1876, Father Baldwin wrote from Lahaina, having just arrived from Honolulu, as follows:

> Oh, how glad I would be to keep on to your home and look in on you and your dear little group and mingle our tears together over the sad affliction which God has appointed to us – nor would we forget to lift up the voice of thanksgiving and praise to our Heavenly father for so signally interposing at the last extremity and saving your life. You will never forget that last instant of peril. Oh, how clear is the goodness of God in this case to you and to us all. What shall we render to him for such mercy?

A letter from Father Baldwin dated the twenty-eighth of April mentioned having heard that Henry was about on horseback. In fact, with his accustomed energy he had plunged again into work, much sooner probably than was wise.

When approaching the mill again for the first time after the accident he is reported to have apostro-

phized it in words which he later made good, as
follows:

> You have handicapped me for life. Now I am going to
> make you support me.

We must return, however, to the building of the
Hamakua Ditch. This project, the pioneer operation of its kind in the Islands, had been for some
time in the minds of Mr. Alexander and Mr. Baldwin. The rain in the Islands is carried by the northeast trade winds and falls on the windward slopes of
the mountains, which are too rough for cultivation,
being cut by large gorges down which the water runs
back to the sea without benefiting man other than by
decorating for him one of the loveliest districts in the
world. The plantations were situated on the level
tracts of land farther to the southeast, upon which
very little rain fell and where in consequence vegeta-
tion did not thrive. With that constructive imagination fundamental in successful captains of industry,
the partners conceived the idea of carrying this water
through tunnel and ditch from the gorges of East
Maui to the potentially fertile but dry lands of Central Maui. Accordingly they commenced negotiations with the government and obtained from it a
lease dated September 30, 1876, by which they were
authorized to build an aqueduct to carry certain water
to the desired territory, but upon condition that the
ditch should be completed by September 30, 1878.

This lease ran in favor of the Haiku Sugar Company (situated to the northeast of Paia and managed
by Mr. Alexander), Alexander and Baldwin, co-
partners, James Alexander and T. H. Hobron (pri-

Samuel Thomas Alexander

121

vate sugar planters), all of whom on November 2, 1876 organized the Hamakua Ditch Company.

The old Haiku plantation record contains the following entry for August 24, 1876:

Mr. A. said that he had had Mr. J. M. Alexander to survey most of the distance, and that according to their views the undertaking was feasible. The estimate for the cost of the ditch was not over $25,000 according to his own ideas. He hoped to be able to bring the water into their fields as early as May 1877, if the grant and water privileges could be obtained from the government.

As it turned out, Mr. Alexander was unduly optimistic, both as to the time for finishing the project and in his estimate of the amount of money which would be needed. In fact, the cost of the ditch was about eighty thousand dollars; and to obtain this sum proved very difficult. It was a new kind of enterprise not then proven successful, and business men timidly shook their heads when it was proposed that they should assist with their capital. In the end Castle and Cooke, agents for the plantations concerned, were persuaded to advance the necessary money, and the work was commenced. Mr. Baldwin then threw himself into the task with his accustomed energy, notwithstanding that he was still so little recovered from his almost fatal accident that during those days in the "ditch country" he was often obliged to ride away into the woods by himself, dismount from his horse and, unseen by the laborers, lie down until rested sufficiently to proceed.

When the ditch builders came to the last great obstacle, the deep gorge of Maliko, it became necessary in connection with the laying of the pipe down and up the sides of the precipices there encountered, for the workmen to lower themselves over the cliffs by rope, hand over hand. This at first they absolutely refused to do. The crisis was serious. Mr. Baldwin met it by himself sliding down the rope, using his legs and his one arm, with which he alternately gripped and released the rope to take a fresh hold lower down. This was done before his injured arm had healed and with a straight fall of two hundred feet to the rocks below! The workmen were so shamed by this exhibition of courage on the part of their one armed manager, that they did not hesitate to follow him down the rope. To keep the heart in them and to watch the progress of the work, Mr. Baldwin day after day went through this dangerous performance.

Before the ditch was completed a new danger appeared. Claus Spreckels, who exerted a great influence over King Kalakaua, obtained on July 8, 1878, a lease of the waters, including those in the section to be traversed by the Hamakua Ditch,

> That are not utilized on or before the date of these presents –
> provided that such grant shall not interfere with prior or
> vested rights of other parties in and to water of said streams
> or on government lands.

This lease made it absolutely essential that the work be completed within the time limit, namely, September 30, 1878, otherwise the water would go to Mr. Spreckels. Unfortunately on July 9, 1878, Samuel Alexander left on a trip to Europe with his brother William, probably not being aware of the lease to Mr. Spreckels, and it was left to Mr. Baldwin, without the help of his partner and without assistance from any trained engineer, to carry the task to completion before his rights should be forfeited.

Mr. Langford, who superintended the work, was, in fact, a carpenter by trade and consulted with Mr. Baldwin about all details, while the overseers (selected from a band of shipwrecked sailors) and the laborers were quite inexperienced in the kind of work required.

At last, as the result of untiring effort, the work was finished, only just in time, but soon enough to give the lie to the dismal prophets who declared that the enterprise must fail and that Spreckels would get the water which Baldwin and Alexander had worked so hard to obtain.

It was a great day on Maui when the water came through the Maliko pipe on the southwestern side of the gulch. When word was brought that the time had come Father Baldwin left Sunnyside for the scene of operations on horseback. Mrs. Baldwin, however, could not endure to be left behind and, securing another horse, followed, using a punuku (noose about the horse's nose) since no bridle was available. She arrived unfortunately just too late to see the water come through the pipes.

This event was extremely puzzling to the natives, who had prophesied freely that not Kamuela (Samuel Alexander), Paluina (Mr. Baldwin), nor any one else could make water flow through a pipe uphill, the principle of the inverted siphon not having at that time penetrated the native mind.

The following excerpts are taken from an account

The Hamakua Ditch Trail

East Maui, Hawaiian Islands

125

of the ditch by F. L. Clarke published in Thrum's
Annual for 1878:

The line, some seventeen miles in extent, with the excep-
tion of a few miles near the plantation, passes through the
dense forest that covers the side of the mountain, and in running the levels for the work many large ravines and innumer-
able small valleys and gulches were encountered. In the
smaller of these the ditch winds its way, with here and there
a flume striding the hollow, while through nine of the larger
the water is carried in pipes twenty-six inches in diameter.

The digging of the ditch was a work of no small magni-
tude. A large gang of men, sometimes numbering two hundred, was employed in the work, and the providing of food,
shelter, tools, etc., was equal to the care of a regiment of
soldiers on the march. As the grade of the ditch gradually
carried the work high up into the woods, cart-roads had to
be surveyed and cut from the main road to the shifting
camps. All the heavy timbers for flumes, etc., were painfully
dragged up hill and down, and in and out of deep gulches,
severely taxing the energies and strength of man and beast,
while the ever-recurring question of a satisfactory food supply
created a demand for everything eatable to be obtained from
the natives within ten miles, besides large supplies drawn
from Honolulu and abroad.

At the head of the work many difficult ledges of rock
were encountered, and blasting and tunneling were resorted
to, to reach the coveted water. While work on the ditch
was thus progressing, pipe makers from San Francisco were
busied riveting together the broad sheets of iron to make the
huge lengths of tube fitted to cross the deep ravines. These
lengths had each to be immersed in a bath of pitch and tar
which coated them inside and out, preserving the iron from
rust, and effectually stopping all minute leaks. The lengths
thus prepared being placed in position in the bottom of the
ravines, the upright lengths were fitted to each other (like
lengths of stove-pipe) with the greatest care, and clamped
firmly to the rocky sides of the cliffs. Their perpendicular

length varies from 90 feet to 450 feet; the greatest being the
pipe that carries the water down into, across, and out of
Maliko gulch to the Baldwin and Alexander Plantations.
At this point every one engaged on the work toiled at the
risk of his life; for the sides of the ravines are almost perpendicular, and a "bed" had to be constructed down these
sides. Then each length of pipe was lowered into the ravine
and placed carefully in position; after which the perpendicular lengths were built up to the brink.

The whole work cannot yet be said to be completed, for
although the water supply was introduced to Haiku's fields
July 4th, 1877, within a year from its inception, it is the aim
of its projectors to continue on the work till it reaches the
Nailiilihaele gulch, thus taking in six principal streams for
their supply, as per grant from government, viz: Honapau,
Holawa, Huelo, Hoalua, Kailua and Nailiilihaele. The ditch
is now as far as Hoalua gulch, and will be continued during
the winter as the weather will permit.

After the construction of the ditch the plantation
had in irrigation a weapon which though not always
effective against drought, was sufficiently so to enable
it to go steadily ahead, while the improved prices for
sugar under reciprocity also helped the situation, and
in time the old hard times were almost forgotten in
the days of plenty and prosperity that followed.

The building of this ditch was an event of the ut-
most significance, not only to the Island of Maui but
to the whole group. In all of the Islands similar
conditions existed, which the progressive planters began to meet in the way which had been shown by
Alexander and Baldwin on Maui. The results on
that Island have been impressive. The Spreckels,
Lowrie, Koolau and other ditches have followed the
Hamakua ditch, and Central Maui, which was once

Sunnyside Home, East Maui in 1883

From left to right: Frank, Maria, Fred, Mrs. Baldwin, Maud, Mr. Baldwin, William, Miss Armstrong, and Arthur Baldwin

a bare waste, is now one of the most productive spots on the globe, supporting a prosperous population where formerly little existed besides the razorback hog, the prickly pear, and wild indigo.

During the six years following the building of the ditch the family lived very happily at the Sunnyside home. How many are the delightful memories which the Baldwin children cherish of those Sunnyside days! Of Fannie, the goat (a male goat, by the way), of games of local invention such as "Mr. Bixby's game" and "Mule," in which Mr. Baldwin used to join occasionally upon his return from work, of the abundant harvests of figs and mulberries, of swimming in the plantation reservoir, of trips to Olinda and many others.

In 1882 an auction was held at which most of the Sunnyside furniture was disposed of, and Mr. and Mrs. Baldwin, accompanied by the children and Cho, Japanese nurse for the baby (Fred), left for San Francisco on the little schooner Anna, Captain McCullough in command, making the voyage from Kahului to the coast in nineteen eventful days. It was a very jolly party, as always happened when "Uncle Charlie Dickey" was present, and to the children no voyage of such surpassing interest has ever been made before or since. Nor did ever explorer behold a more entrancing sight than did they when they awoke one morning to find the Anna anchored in the Bay of San Francisco with its ferryboats, tugs, sailing ships, steamers, and its cities perched high on the surrounding hills.

A house was rented on Vallejo Street in San Francisco and all the children except Frank, aged four, and Fred, aged only a very little, attended the Jackson Street School. Harry Baldwin's eighteen-dollar suit, adventures and fights with Tom Canty, the drunkard's son, excursions with Mrs. Baldwin to Woodword's Gardens (now Golden Gate Park), the Cliff House, and the Presidio, the "snow storm" of 1882 which more nearly resembled a snow storm than anything San Francisco had seen for many years, these are all matters of which pleasant memories will long remain.

Mr. Baldwin shortly after arriving in San Francisco, left with his friend, William H. Bailey, for a trip to Louisiana and elsewhere in the South and then returned to Maui whence he came back in 1883 to bring the family home on the old steamer Suez.

Shortly after the return of the family to Sunnyside, he accepted the management of the Haiku plantation in place of Mr. Samuel Alexander, who had resigned on account of ill health and had moved to California. Mr. E. M. Walsh was made manager of the Paia plantation in place of Mr. Baldwin.

In the meantime Mr. Baldwin had become financially interested in the Haiku as well as the Paia plantation. It is interesting now to note in the old records of the former that in 1877 Mr. Alexander discussed with its board a plan "for the new mill to be constructed on the west side of Maliko Gulch" (the Hamakuapoko mill). Later in 1877 it was decided to offer the plantation to Spreckels at the bottom price of five hundred thousand dollars (a deal that fortunately was never consummated). In 1881

130

The Haiku Home

Maui, Hawaiian Islands

Mr. Baldwin bought his first fifty shares of its stock and was shortly afterwards elected its vice-president.

More of the family memories and history are connected with the beautiful old home at Haiku than even at Sunnyside, its earliest home, or Maluhia, its latest.

Mr. Baldwin, however, was almost too active a man to enjoy his home, working as he did with the most intense energy, being in the saddle at four or five in the morning and often riding twenty or twenty-five miles before breakfast, after which he would be off again for the rest of the day.

And yet we remember how of an evening he would send for a group of music lovers with their various instruments and among them would come limping in old Schneider, the tanner, with his violin. Then, himself playing his reed organ (using his feet for the bass parts), they would enjoy a feast of music which no doubt drove black care over the hills and far away.

On the Sabbath also did all thought of plantations, business, debt, and care take flight from the household. On that day, strictly observed though it was, the family came closer together. The father had then time to manifest the love and affection for his children, which throughout his life was one of his leading motives, and what a rock of comfort and strength he was!

Sunday morning began with prayer, followed after breakfast by study of the coming Sunday School lesson with Mrs. Baldwin, a short interval while horses and carriages were being got ready, after which the children usually on horseback and the elders by carriage (which it was a great honor to the youngsters to be permitted to drive), all would go some five miles to the old Makawao church where the country-side met, exchanged gossip, and worshiped together. Homeward bound, how the boys enjoyed to fly their ponies over the ditch at Kaluanui and what excitement when driving to pass, if one could, the Dickey's buggy drawn by the fleet footed Hector, a Young Venture colt! In fact the question of the superiority of Hector to the Baldwins' Dick, Katy C., and Black Bess has not been to this day settled to the satisfaction of both families.

Sunday afternoons the neighbors, the Dickeys and the Beckwiths, with their guests would usually gather in one house or the other for a "sing" and bad little boys who didn't want to take part found it generally expedient to attend.

Those were the Sundays of pleasant memories. But Monday came around in Haiku as inevitably as it does elsewhere. Then the children would go back to the little private school in the Haiku grounds, and their father from early morning until nightfall to his work on the plantation.

The Haiku Sugar Company was then heavily in debt to its agents, Castle and Cooke. The land on the windward side of Maliko Gulch was becoming exhausted. A great fire destroyed the "Trash House" at Haiku. Notwithstanding these and other troubles, in a very few years Mr. Baldwin had the plantation out of debt and for the first time since its start in 1858, paying dividends, an achievement which immediately placed him in the first rank of Hawaiian plantation managers.

These results were achieved partly through the manager's never failing energy and partly by his sagacity in abandoning the old Haiku mill (built in 1861) and substituting in its place and in place of the Haiku lands the mill and lands at Hamakuapoko. With increasing prosperity, more and more lands, including that of the neighboring plantations, were taken over and the theatre of operations moved steadily southward away from Haiku.

The old mill at Haiku became in time a picturesque ruin and the Haiku cane-fields grazing land and a wonderful playground for the Baldwin children, who found frequent occasion to lasso the harmless horses and cattle pastured there. Sometimes, be it said with shame, when their father was far away, they would ride to the remote districts of Mahuwa and Kuiaha and rope and unrope the unhappy steers without even the pretense of an excuse (a crime now first openly confessed).

The cattle and horse ranch, however, though to the boys the most important part of the plantation, was one of its least significant features to Mr. Baldwin, who concentrated his attention upon the mill and the cane-fields, not worrying much about what befell in Haiku when his back was turned. While the children played, he worked with hardly a respite until in 1887 he went on a well-earned vacation trip with his brother-in-law, Samuel M. Damon, to England where he saw the Queen's Jubilee.

During the active and prosperous years which followed, he began more and more to engage in public affairs. In those days the government of the kingdom had fallen upon evil days and "the wicked flourished like a green bay tree." The better elements were compelled to take action. Mr. Baldwin, whose inclinations were against public life, joined the movement with great reluctance and solely from a sense of duty, but once in the fight for clean politics, he was never again out of it. The steps which led him to take part are told as follows by his old friend, Mr. W. R. Castle:

It was resolved to make a strong fight for the election of honest and progressive members of the Legislature for the session opening in April, 1886, and in the latter part of the year 1885 I was sent to look over the field and confer with different influential people on the Islands about the prospects, and what sort of assistance could be expected. On Maui I was asked more particularly to see Mr. Baldwin and went out at once to Paia. He was living at that time in the old Haiku Plantation house. When he was ready to go home to dinner, we started for Haiku. The conversation on the road was memorable. We talked first of old days, then of business matters, changes in Honolulu, the conduct of Kalakaua since he had been made King, and various other matters of like nature. I was extremely interested in Mr. Baldwin's cautious view of public questions then pending. He did not state definitely just what his attitude would be on the proposed progressive or reform campaign, but tried to inform himself as to the opinions of business men in Honolulu, who had become stirred up by the condition of things to the point when they had determined to make a move. It was evident that he felt that there had been too much apathy on political matters. At the same time he stated plainly that he was averse to adopting measures which would have a tendency to destroy the Hawaiian Monarchy, but appeared to be entirely satisfied with the attitude of business

135

Henry Perrine Baldwin

At the age of about 45

people in Honolulu, which was thoroughly loyal to the existing government but determined that the unscrupulous ambition of the King should be curbed, and that the government must be carried on honestly, economically and in the interest of the governed, and not for the supposed amusement of Kalakaua. He expressed himself as in sympathy with that attitude and with those opinions but seemed unwilling to add to his other very heavy cares, the responsibility of a campaign on Maui. There is no question but that he held very progressive, vigorous and decided views on public questions and was averse to the adoption of any measure which would tend to overthrow the historic Hawaiian Monarchy. We agreed on those points and, after some further interviews with others, I returned to Honolulu.

The King was triumphant in that Election and the Legislature showed only nine Reform members, the rest, outside of the House of Nobles, being all candidates pledged to support David Kalakaua in any measure that he might wish to have introduced. From letters written by Mr. Baldwin to members of the Legislature and comments by himself when in town, it is evident that he took a very strong interest in what was going on, though he still persisted in refusing to take any public position.

The prorogation of this Legislature was followed by the organization of what was known as the "Hawaiian League." It was called revolutionary, but an organization to procure, if possible, and insist upon government by constitutional means, can hardly be called revolutionary. There was a very strong element in the league determined to bring about annexation to the United States, but prior to the mass meeting which finally resulted in a revolution, by which Kalakaua was compelled to give a new and more liberal constitution, this annexation element, after a long and very bitter discussion, was defeated and the Hawaiians, meaning thereby those of Hawaiian birth, parentage and affiliation, procured a promise on the part of the league that its attempts would be confined to a reformed Hawaiian government, under sufficient guaranties to insure responsible and safe government.

The promulgation of the Constitution of 1887, was followed immediately by an election in which Mr. Baldwin consented to stand for election as a representative of the Reform Party, and he then became a member of the first Reform Legislature, which had two sessions, the special session of 1887 and the regular session of 1888.

Those were very troublous times. Race feeling engendered by the Revolution of 1887 was very bitter. The king and his partisans attempted to pass such bills as those providing for opium licenses and the removal of restrictions on the sale of liquor to Hawaiians, measures which were opposed by the members of the Reform Party, including among their numbers some of the best men of the kingdom.

Mr. Baldwin served in that session and almost continuously thereafter on the Foreign Relations Committee, a very important body. In subsequent sessions he served on the Finance Committee and on numerous special committees. In connection with his work on the Foreign Relations Committee, during this session of 1887 he brought in a minority report severely condemning the participants in the notorious London Loan affair, which was authorized by the corrupt Legislature of 1886. Among other activities he introduced a bill making it unlawful to sell liquor at retail outside of Honolulu. Though passed, this bill was vetoed by the king.

Says Mr. W. R. Castle:

His ability, really amounting to genius, in financial matters was felt in measures, suggested by his committee, which became law. Mr. Baldwin also introduced a measure with regard to the age for compulsory education providing that

138

only pupils over thirteen years of age, who could pass certain examinations, should be allowed to engage in manual labor. While this bill was defeated at that time, it was wise and just and has since been recognized and incorporated in the laws of the country and regulations of the Board of Education.

From 1887 to 1903, he was continuously a member of the upper house of the Legislature, known as the House of Nobles under the Monarchy, and the Senate under the Republic and the territorial form of government. During this period he commanded to an unusual degree the confidence of the natives. Notwithstanding the bad feeling which often prevailed, he was only once defeated in his campaigns for re-election. Throughout his service in the Legislature he rendered invaluable service as a great reconciler of the various factions. No one was a better or more sincere friend to the Hawaiians, a fact which they themselves always recognized. Fortunate it was that the man whom they so trusted should have been of sterling Christian character, wise and of great breadth of view and sympathy.

An indication of the sort of thing that had to be met in those legislatures may be gathered from the following petitions on the burning question of leprosy treatment presented to the Legislature in 1889:

1. That the present board of health be removed.

2. That a board be appointed that will show more kindness in the way of doing business.

3. That persons who profess to be able to cure leprosy be allowed the opportunity to do so.

4. That people be prohibited from taking crabs, etc., from the reef opposite the leper settlement.

5. That Dr. Emerson be prohibited from the practice of medicine in the Kingdom.

Also the following:

1. That the taking of lepers to Kalawao be discontinued.
2. That all lepers be allowed to return to their homes.
3. That the board of health be disbanded.
4. That everybody be allowed to doctor the lepers.

The universal testimony is that his rare combination of tact and firmness did excellent work during this period, in holding in check his more radical and often ignorant colleagues. This was of vital importance in defeating the opium and lottery rings and all the intrigues engaged in by the unscrupulous adventurers of those days.

At the time of the Wilcox Revolution in 1889, and of the attempt of the king in 1890 to assemble a convention with a view to restoring some of the royal prerogatives of the old constitution, Mr. Baldwin, according to Dr. William D. Alexander, was a great "moderating influence and balance wheel" and helped materially in the defeat of this dangerous project. No doubt if there had been many more like him engaged in public affairs, there would have been less talk of missionary and anti-missionary, of haole and anti-haole.

The session of 1891 was an exceedingly stormy one. The recently organized National Reform Party, which was earnestly opposed to reform, swept the boards clean on every Island except Maui and Kauai. On Maui Mr. Baldwin and C. H. Dickey were the only Reform (opposed to the National Reform Party) candidates elected. When the Legislature assem-

Life and Character

bled, Thurston, minister of the interior, accused his colleague C. W. Ashford, the attorney general, of conspiring with V. V. Ashford and "Bob" Wilcox to organize an insurrection for the purpose of restoring the king to his former power. The majority of the Committee on Foreign Affairs retorted by charging ministers Austin, Thurston, and Damon (all of the Reform Party) with endeavoring through the proposed Treaty of 1889 to lay the foundations for annexation of the Islands to the United States. The reform ministry was then voted out of office. Mr. Baldwin brought in a minority report for the Foreign Affairs Committee which was thus characterized by the *Hawaiian Gazette* of that time:

> The minority report of the Foreign Affairs Committee presented by Noble Baldwin, the full text of which has been published in these columns, is in many ways one of the most notable reports which has been presented to the Legislature. The situation was a peculiar one. The majority report was a violent partizan document, not merely abusive in its terms, but actually unparliamentary in its language. Under these circumstances it would have been no wonder if the minority report had shown something of the same want of temper and measure. But nothing of these qualities is visible in this report, which is conspicuous by its moderation, fairness, and candor. The report amounts, indeed, to a complete vindication of the foreign policy of the late ministry, but it is so, not through any ingenious or elaborate argumentation, but because it is a calm, complete objective statement of the facts.

To return now to business matters: it is interesting to recall that about this time Mr. Claus Spreckels tried urgently to induce Mr. Baldwin to approve of the consolidation of the Haiku, Paia, and Hawaiian Commercial plantations (the last being controlled by

The old Hamakuapoko Mill, Maui

Mr. Baldwin in the foreground

Mr. Spreckels). Mr. Baldwin was to be made manager of the immense plantation which would result from the combination, and was almost persuaded. No doubt he was always glad that he finally declined the proposition.

In the summer of 1889 he went with his wife and three oldest children, with members of the families of Messrs. S. T. Alexander and J. B. Atherton, to England and continental Europe.

While in Scotland he met Messrs. W. R. Watson and E. M. Walsh and arranged with them for an assignment of a lease held by them on a part of the Gay and Robinson lands on Kauai to a new plantation incorporated on October 30, 1889 as the Hawaiian Sugar Company.

A few years after this event and before the necessary preliminary improvements had been made, or all the money therefor called in from the stockholders, the McKinley Tariff Bill was passed by the United States Congress, putting sugar on the free list, and thus nullifying to the islands the advantages of the reciprocity treaty. The era of rather extravagant prosperity which had prevailed for several years in the Hawaiian sugar industry suddenly ceased. The price of sugar fell at first to the extent of two cents a pound. Dividends were passed and rigid systems of economy were put in practice. Lessons were thus learned from which the Islands have ever since benefited.

At this time the stockholders of the Hawaiian Sugar Company, although they had already paid in a part of their subscriptions, being frightened at the gloomy outlook ahead were not inclined to proceed with the enterprise. Mr. Baldwin, however, was not discouraged. He persuaded the stockholders to stand by the new plantation, assuring them that he would not call for more than seventy per cent of their subscriptions. This promise he kept notwithstanding the building of an immense irrigation ditch, a large diffusion mill, and other improvements. To supply his part of this subscription, Mr. Baldwin himself went heavily into debt to J. D. Spreckels and Brothers of San Francisco, a debt which was long a burden, and even a danger.

The Hanapepe Ditch of the Hawaiian Sugar Company, built in 1890 and 1891, like the Hamakua Ditch on Maui, is a lasting monument to Mr. Baldwin's ability and energy. Both were laid out in large part by him and although he had had no technical education as a civil engineer, both are remarkable examples of engineering skill. In fact, Mr. Allardt, a California engineer of excellent reputation, having been engaged to look over the plans for the Hanapepe Ditch before construction was commenced, reported he could suggest no improvements of importance.

In 1891 occurred the death of King Kalakaua. With all his faults he had many of the kindly characteristics of his race, and his relations with Mr. Baldwin were not unfriendly, notwithstanding the latter's frequent political opposition. The king in fact often invited him to the palace and manifested appreciation of his friendship for the Hawaiians by appointing him to the order of Kulia.

Upon the accession of Queen Liliuokalani it was

hoped that an era of good feeling had been inaugurated. Early in her reign, at Haiku Mr. Baldwin gave a great *luau* [native feast] in her honor. There were present more than two thousand persons and a great quantity of meats, vegetables, and delicacies was cooked (and eaten) in the old Hawaiian fashion. Mr. Baldwin made a happy speech in the Hawaiian language, and there were eloquent responses from the natives present, all full of good feeling, notwithstanding that many of the orators had previously expressed the most violent sentiments against the whites, the missionaries, and the like. Such was the kindly influence of food and hospitality.

Later when the affairs of the unfortunate queen reached a crisis and the city of Honolulu was aroused and determined to depose her from the throne, Mr. Baldwin standing practically alone among the men of his party, addressed the people urging that only such means should be adopted as were "within the Constitution." This speech, however, fell upon deaf ears and seeing that he was hopelessly in the minority he gave up his attempt to moderate the passion of the hour.

Nevertheless, upon the establishment of the Provisional Government in 1893, he became one of its most substantial adherents and was relied upon by members of the government for his wise counsel and because of the influence which he commanded, especially on the Island of Maui.

In this year of 1893, there was much in business to occupy his attention. The McKinley Bill was then passed with the almost distastrous result to the sugar

Henry Perrine Baldwin

At about the age of 50

industry already mentioned; and Mr. Baldwin was obliged to work very hard to keep his plantations alive until prosperity should return.

About this time, Mr. Morrison, manager of the Hawaiian Sugar Company, was obliged, on account of ill health, to take a long vacation, and Mr. Baldwin moved with his family to Makaweli Kauai to take personal charge of that plantation. The situation there was serious. The diffusion process in the mill was not proving successful. It was necessary to eliminate the discontent which prevailed among the higher employees. These months which he spent on Kauai were some of the hardest and most wearing of his life. At the end he turned over a much improved plantation to Mr. Morrison upon the latter's return from Scotland.

A memorable part of the Kauai visit was a trip which Mr. and Mrs. Baldwin took behind a four horse team, accompanied by the writer of this memoir around the Island of Kauai. On the way they spent a delightful night with the Rice family at Lihue. At Hanalei, their journey's end, they revisited the old Waioli house, Father Alexander's first home in the Hawaiian Islands. It was a day full of reminiscences of the early missionary life.

An incident of the Kauai residence, very characteristic of Mr. Baldwin, occurred as follows: the writer having been invited by Mr. Francis Gay to shoot an occasional wild turkey on the Gay and Robinson lands, one day came upon a flock of the birds while riding with Mr. Baldwin up the side of Koulu Valley. The sportsman in Mr. Baldwin which no

147

amount of business or politics could quite suppress immediately conquered all else. Crying out "Arthur, let me see what I can do!" he took the shot gun and, one-armed as he was, straightway brought down a fine large turkey.

It now seems strange that we did not in those days marvel at his ability to do most things as well with one arm as other people did with two. For example, in this matter of shooting, he used to take his young sons on trips of happy memory to the mountain house at Olinda, and on the turkey hunts that ensued would often bring down his bird from horseback. Riding the high spirited horses he loved, he would take the reins in his teeth and open the heaviest of gates without dismounting; and to mount such horses without help seemed to him not difficult at all. When the family moved up the mountain to Olinda, he would carry a child seated on a pillow in front of his saddle and it occurred to no one to doubt that he could manage the business safely. His facility in dressing himself and preparing his meat and other food seems now remarkable. One of his daughters recalls how once when she could not remove a splinter from his hand, he had her hold the needle while he himself so operated his hand as to succeed where she had failed. A thousand such anecdotes might be told.

In the latter part of 1893, Mr. Baldwin with his family returned to Haiku, bringing with him, among other things, the white-faced Arabian pony, Bowery, which later was closely associated with the memory of his dearly loved son Fred.

In 1892 and 1893, there was built the Baldwin

Life and Character

Home at the Leper Settlement on the Island of Molokai. His old friend Brother Dutton, for many years, and at this writing, the true and faithful superintendent of the Baldwin Home says:

Father Damien began gathering some boys early in 1886. So when I came, in July, he had about fifteen, living in little huts around his house. Some of them might be called cabins. Soon we had about fifty boys and men. Two larger buildings were put up and the inmates increased rapidly in number.

Hon. H. P. Baldwin was eager to provide the home for boys and men, a home well constructed and convenient.

The first general construction of the Home was all paid for by Mr. Baldwin and he often invited me to call upon him for anything new or additional that might be needed.

Counting the living, we have had at the Baldwin Home 1073 inmates. We aim to operate the home as a big family – the largest on the Island.

The "outside" people, as all not in the homes are called, are always about two-thirds of the total. They live in families, part families, etc., etc. In the homes there are advantages and the opportunity for control, that would be impossible "outside."

How much good has been done in Bishop and Baldwin Homes – as to morals in general, as to sober living, in the building up of good character, in becoming accustomed to work of various sorts, no living person can estimate.

At Kalaupapa (the Bishop Home for Girls), the present management has made many improvements, better buildings, some regularity as to streets, etc.

Still for beauty, there is no peer to Baldwin Home. All who speak of it tell me this. I have not been away from Baldwin Home yard for nearly twenty years.

Mr. Baldwin's marked success as a manager is well known. To know his charities in like manner they must be searched out. This of the leper settlement that we have given his name, was a favorite with him. He told me so the last time I

149

The Leper Settlement at Kalawao,
Molokai, Hawaiian Islands

In the Foreground

The Baldwin Home for Boys

saw him. His cheerful disposition had already added much to his ever ready help. The evident value of the work in the higher sense, gave him pleasure, and I hope it may always be so to the Baldwin family, and to all of us here, with God's blessing.

The increasing pressure of his public and philanthropic enterprises induced Mr. Baldwin in the Fall of 1893 to make Mr. J. W. Colville, who had formerly been manager of the Paia plantation, manager also of the Haiku plantation, while he himself retained the position of general manager. This position, one of general oversight over these plantations and the others in which he was interested, leaving many of the details to the managers, including later his sons Harry and Frank, he continued to occupy under different designations for the rest of his life.

In 1894 he formed a partnership with his brother-in-law, Samuel T. Alexander, under the name of Alexander and Baldwin which in 1900 was incorporated under the name of Alexander and Baldwin, Limited. The firm was at first the San Francisco agency for the Haiku and Paia plantations only. In 1897 a Honolulu branch was established and the agency of the plantations transferred to it from the old firm of Castle and Cooke. Starting from a small beginning, the new firm at once set for itself an inflexibly high standard of business morality. Obligations were faithfully and promptly met. That such policies pay was manifested in the firm's steadily increasing business. Its further history is largely a history of Mr. Baldwin himself.

In 1894 he was a member of the convention which

was called to establish a Hawaiian Republic, serving on its executive and finance committees.

Under the Republic then inaugurated, he continued to be an active and influential member of the Legislature. Among other measures which he supported was the Land Act of 1895, which was framed in the interest of the small proprietors rather than of his own class.

Judge S. B. Dole, then president of the republic, writing of this period, says:

> In those days he was often in my room at the Capitol on matters of public business, and always showed a desire to reach the bottom of propositions for legislation, and to act for the public interests. During the political disturbances of 1895, he was a helpful counsellor and ever maintained a cheerful optimism. I well remember his expedition for information at the time of the uprising of 1895. In one of the smaller coasting steamers he proceeded to several ports of Maui and Hawaii with instructions to land and communicate by telephone or otherwise with the available sources of information and obtain all possible data as to the political condition of those islands in relation to the uprising in Honolulu. He performed this mission quickly and with such discretion that his visits hardly provoked a ripple of excitement in those communities.

At this time, when the Island of Maui was cut off from communication with the outside world, all that the family knew of this mysterious trip was that H. P. Baldwin had landed at Makena for a few minutes one night from the little steamer Keauhou and from there had gone to the Island of Hawaii. Its natural anxiety, however, was set at rest some days later when the Honolulu authorities permitted the resumption of interisland navigation.

Henry Perrine Baldwin

At about the age of 55

Life and Character

During these years his charitable enterprises were constantly increasing. The Makawao Church was rebuilt at Paliuli on the site of the original Paia sugar-mill. Of this church Mr. Baldwin was always a faithful member, attending its services regularly, and contributing liberally to its financial needs. The East Maui Seminary for Hawaiian girls, having been burned to the ground, was rebuilt near the old Sunnyside home. In this institution, always a favorite with him, he constantly showed the most eager interest. The native Hawaiian ministers on the Island of Maui were supported, in large part, by him, and the interest of the Protestant and other churches aided in many ways. He rebuilt his father's old church at Wainee. Numerous young men were sent at his expense to school and college. His benefactions, in fact, were very large and were not usually known even to his own family.

Almost every morning at Haiku there would be two or three natives waiting for a word with him as he came out from breakfast to mount his horse. What passed between him and these old fellows we shall never know, but notwithstanding the pressure of his affairs he always seemed to find time to talk and advise with them, and never ceased in his *aloha* [love] for their race.

This feeling is perhaps best expressed by him in his own words, uttered on September 2, 1902, when putting Prince Kuhio in nomination as Republican candidate for delegate to Congress. We quote from the *Hawaiian Gazette* of the following day:

In his nominating speech Mr. Baldwin said that he took

154

great pleasure in announcing as his choice for delegate a prince of the royal family of Hawaii. "I repeat," said he, "that it is a great privilege to offer the name of Prince Kalanianaole. I had my sixtieth birthday just a few days ago —"

"We hope you will have sixty more," interposed Delegate B. T. Guard, of Hilo, the members of the convention approving the sentiment with long applause.

Mr. Baldwin, continuing said, "As we grow older we do not, as a rule, celebrate our birthdays with the same gusto as when we were fifteen or sixteen years of age. I may say, though, that I spent the first fifty-one years of my life under the Hawaiian monarchy and the last nine years under other forms of government culminating in that of a Territory of the Republic of the United States.

"I cannot forget the pleasure of the years I lived under the monarchy, as a youth, as a young man, as a man of business. My remembrances of all those days give me a heartfelt aloha for Hawaii and the Hawaiians.

"But it is idle to look backward. We are entering upon a new era, an era full of large possibilities to these Islands. We are looking for a glorious outcome to the Hawaiian Islands as a branch of the great United States government.

"Now, I state that I nominate the Prince with a genuine aloha for himself and his native fellow-countrymen. The Republican party here should be proud that it is to have in its ranks a leader of the Hawaiians who has declared himself a Republican. I believe that the Prince himself should be proud that he has chosen to belong to that party, which is a party that stands for the good of the whole people."

In 1899 the Kihei lands near Maalaea Bay on Maui, of which Mr. Baldwin was one of the owners, were turned over to the new Kihei Plantation Company, Mr. Baldwin receiving for his share of the land eight hundred ninety-one thousand dollars par value of the stock, besides which he subscribed in cash for a considerable amount. These lands were naturally fertile but were situated in an exceedingly dry district. The plan was to bring water to them by means of wells and pumps, as had already been done successfully at Ewa on Oahu. Mr. Baldwin assumed the presidency and worked hard but unsuccessfully to make the proposition a success. Often three or four times a week, he would ride his horse twenty miles to Kihei, spend the day there, and ride back at nightfall twenty miles to Haiku. Becoming convinced at last that he had received too large an amount of stock for his land in the boom period of the plantation's beginnings, he insisted on surrendering to the company four hundred forty-five thousand, five hundred dollars par value, equal to one-half of the stock given him for his land. Notwithstanding this unprecedented and generous action and despite the labor and thought that had been expended upon it, it became necessary in the end to abandon Kihei as a separate plantation.

Following upon the starting of the Kihei plantation, Mr. Baldwin's next enterprise was in connection with the already existing Hawaiian Commercial and Sugar Company. In 1898 the control of this plantation, which had been first with Mr. Claus Spreckels, and later, after some litigation, with his sons, was secured by Mr. Pollitz, a San Francisco stockbroker. The latter proceeded at once to Honolulu and offered an option on a controlling block of the stock to Mr. James B. Castle of Honolulu. The option was accepted and Mr. Baldwin and his associates of Alexander and Baldwin were included in the syndicate then formed to take over this stock, Mr. Castle becoming a partner of the firm of Alexander and Baldwin, Limited. From that time until his death Mr. Baldwin was the dominant personality in the affairs of the Hawaiian Commercial and Sugar Company. It had always been his dream, thus realized by the acquisition of this property with the others in which he was already interested, to see that great district of Central Maui with its possibilities of fertility and productiveness, understood by none so well as himself, grow and prosper under his guiding hand.

It did so grow and prosper, but not without years of anxiety and trial. The Hawaiian Commercial Company had never succeeded under its old management, and did not succeed under the new until the year 1902, when Mr. Baldwin took personal charge in place of Mr. Lowrie. At that time the debt of the plantation had increased to a dangerous degree. Its credit with the banks was almost gone. Its fields were "weedy," the laborers discontented, the expense heavy. In a year's time, the plantation under Mr. Baldwin's management had paid off a debt of eight hundred thousand dollars and was on a dividend-paying basis. Conditions surrounding employees were greatly improved and their loyalty and confidence in the management restored. This was one of Mr. Baldwin's greatest commercial successes. On the sentimental side, however, it involved the abandonment of the old Haiku home, which was not again regularly occupied by the family.

Shortly after the taking over of the control of the Hawaiian Commercial and Sugar Company by the so-called Alexander and Baldwin interests, the Hawai-

Looking across central Maui to Haleakala

ian Islands in 1898 were made a part of the United
States, an event of the greatest commercial as well as
political significance to the Islands.   To industry
this meant a stable government and the end of all fear
of the imposition of a duty on Hawaiian sugar going
into the United States.   With these benefits came also
certain burdens, including the shutting off of that
great source of labor supply to the Pacific, the eastern
part of Asia.

Upon annexation, moreover, the planters became
considerably distressed about the possibility of dis-
turbance due to the coming change from the system
of contract labor which had prevailed up to that time
(rather against the desires of such progressive planters as Mr. Baldwin) to the system prevailing in the
United States.   What would the many thousands of
Japanese laborers do upon being suddenly and automatically freed from the obligation of their contracts?   The readjustment was made with considerable difficulty on some of the Maui plantations on
which the managers were not on the best of terms
with their employees.   On the Haiku and Paia plantations, however, the change was accomplished without any difficulty whatever.   All nationalities among
that polyglot collection of laborers trusted Mr. Baldwin implicity.   The Japanese on the Hawaiian Commercial and Sugar Plantation having started a strike
sent to their friends on the Haiku and Paia Plantations to inquire if Mr. Baldwin was *polalei* [to be
trusted], and receiving a favorable answer, they too
were satisfied and the strike was discontinued.   This
was typical of Mr. Baldwin's relations with the Jap-

anese and other laborers through his whole business career. He was always square, always just and although he did not allow imposition and had little use for a loafer, he treated his people well and made them as comfortable as possible in their homes. The result was that at no time did he have really serious labor difficulties on his plantations.

At the close both of Governor Dole's and Governor Carter's administrations, he was urged to be a candidate for the governorship. There was little doubt but that he would have secured the appointment if he had consented, as it was generally said that his was the one nomination which would meet with universal approval. He declined, however, feeling that with his ever increasing business cares and his advancing years it would be impossible for him to accept.

He was also led to this decision because of the fact that, in order to carry out his various business enterprises he had by the year 1900 accumulated a large debt. He had come to the conclusion that he must devote himself to freeing himself from this obligation, an object which after years of consistent effort he finally accomplished. Nevertheless he was able to spare considerable time for his various political duties, although not after 1903 holding any office under the government. He was thenceforth always a member of the Republican Campaign Committee for the Island of Maui, and always felt personal responsibility that the Island should "go Republican." New business enterprises, however, he consistently refused to go into, believing that he must first get out of debt before undertaking any others.

From January 1902 until May 1906, he continued in the personal management of the Hawaiian Commercial and Sugar Company at the same time maintaining a general oversight over the other Alexander and Baldwin plantations, as well as the Haleakala and Honolua cattle ranches.

These were years of great business activity. Most of the plantations in which he was interested undertook extensive improvements calculated to render their positions more secure in case of bad times to come. Chief among these were the Lowrie Ditch undertaken by the Hawaiian Commercial and Sugar Company in 1900, the Koolau Ditch undertaken by the combined East Maui plantations in 1903 and 1904, the Olokele Ditch, built by the Hawaiian Sugar Company in 1902 to 1904, and the new mills which were built at Paia, Makaweli, and Puunene (the Hawaiian Commercial and Sugar Company). Mr. Baldwin was not only a moving spirit in all of these improvements, but took an important part in the general affairs of the sugar planters of all the Islands. In 1904 he was one of the organizers of the Sugar Factors Company, and also helped in the various activities of the Sugar Planters Association, such as its very successful agricultural experiment station and on several occasions he represented the Hawaiian planters in their negotiations with the sugar refiners of the East.

One of his typical busy days is thus described by one of his sons:

I remember on one occasion he left Maui in the afternoon by the "James Makee," for Honolulu, arriving there the

The modern Mill of the
Hawaiian Commercial and Sugar Company
at Puunene

next morning about ten o'clock. He attended to some business there and returned the same afternoon about three o'clock on one of the small boats, the "Iwalani," I think it was, arriving at Kihei on the following morning. There he got a horse from Mr. Pogue, who was then manager of the Kihei Plantation, rode over the Kihei Plantation, arriving at my house at Paliuli, just above the Paia Church. He had lunch with us, got a fresh horse, rode over to Hamakuapoko and looked over the fields and mill. He then rode over to Haiku and got another horse and rode up to Olinda, arriving there about half past six that evening. After dinner, so I am told, he sat up until about half past nine, apparently "as fresh as a daisy."

Only those who have experienced the sleeplessness and discomfort of travel on the smaller interisland steamers and have ridden over those great areas of plantation, some twenty miles in length, will appreciate how strenuous a day this was.

In those active days, if any one remonstrated with him for continuing to work so hard when he had earned the right to leisure if any man ever had, he would reply "I would rather wear out than rust out." The wearing process, however, although he would never admit it, began somewhat to gain upon him. Beginning with the year 1905, he was subjected to a series of shocks which in the end seriously impaired his strength. First came a heavy and unexpected blow in the death of his son, Fred, which occurred in New York, October 11, 1905. This son had spent much of his time with his parents in the home at Maluhia on Maui, and full as he was of life, activity, and promise, his loss left a void in the home which could not be filled. A few months later, Mr. Baldwin was obliged to undergo a severe operation for

163

mastoiditis which was performed in Honolulu by Doctor McDonough of Toronto. His former vitality and strength seemed never afterwards to have been fully recovered.

He wrote at this time to his friend Bishop Restarick of Honolulu:

> MY DEAR BISHOP: Your good kind letter of Sympathy was received while I was at the Hospital in Honolulu and has not been forgotten. Letters of sympathy when one is laid low touch the heart in a tender spot and *cannot* be forgotten.
>
> The blow seemed severe to me, but I feel it was needed to bring me to a full realization of how much I and my family have been prospered under Divine Providence and care, and to bring me to a higher sense of my duties to God and my fellow men.
>
> The lesson will not be forgotten.

Writing to the author of this memoir Bishop Restarick comments:

> To me this letter reveals more clearly than anything else, the real humility and trust of your Father. All great men, or men that I should esteem great, are humble when you get below the surface of the routine in which they must assert themselves, and I think that this letter shows the true spirit of your Father.

That he himself had perceived some loss of his strength appears in his letter of May, 1906 to William G. Cooke, secretary of the Hawaiian Commercial and Sugar Company, stating that he thought it well to anticipate a step which he had intended to take in the following year, namely to immediately resign his position as manager, adding: "The serious time I have been through, it seems to me, is a

Emily Alexander Baldwin

warning voice that it is time for me to step out of the direct management."

Symptoms of the trouble which later caused his death were first noticed about this time. In search of better health he went in 1907 with his wife and daughter, Charlotte, to Japan. The trip was a happy one, but his health did not improve.

He continued, nevertheless, upon his return to follow the affairs of the various plantations very closely, being still in the saddle or automobile a great part of the day. In January of 1909, however, he was taken with an attack of appendicitis and was barely saved by an operation performed by Dr. James R. Judd at the Puunene Hospital. In the summer of that year he went with Mrs. Baldwin on his last trip east. Among other places his travels included a very delightful expedition with Mrs. Baldwin and his son, Arthur, to the Muskoka Lake Region of Canada. His health was noticeably less vigorous than formerly at this time, and business and other cares seemed to disturb him more than ever before. Nevertheless, such was his love of natural beauty and of travel, his keen interest in all the affairs of the world, that he seemed thoroughly to enjoy the excursion.

Before he returned to Maui, the people of that Island held an election and for the first time in years rejected the Republican Party at the polls, a result which he attributed in part to his absence and for which he very severely blamed himself. He stated then that never again would he be absent from the Island at election time.

In the summer of 1910 an election was held in the

Life and Character

Islands at the instance of the American Congress, to ascertain whether the sentiment of the people was for or against the prohibition of the sale of liquor. Mr. Baldwin with all his old time vigor plunged into the fight on behalf of the prohibition cause, notwithstanding that he felt that it was unwise to have precipitated the issue at that time. Among other things he gave a great *luau* [feast] served to several thousand persons at Paia and himself spoke in Hawaiian on behalf of the cause. This combined with the labor of the preparation of the materials for the feast (he always himself followed such matters down to the smallest detail) resulted in a serious sickness. When barely recovered, he was out again, never sparing himself, making speeches and attending meetings until the end of the campaign which resulted, to his chagrin, in the complete success of the "wet" interests.

During the remaining two years of his life, while continuing to be active in business, politics, and philanthropy, he left to some extent the business details to his sons and others. More of his time was given to the enjoyment of his home at Maluhia (built in 1903), where he took the greatest delight in the planting and raising of fruit trees and flowers. It was always one of his keenest pleasures to own and develop a home and grounds upon the heights or mountainside as at Maluhia or Olinda, from whence he would never tire of the view of the hills, cane fields, and plantation villages of Central Maui and beyond over the waters of the Pacific Ocean to the Islands of Kohoolawe, Lanai, and Molokai. That was his coun-

The Home at Maluhia

Maui, Hawaiian Islands

try, the country to which he had given the best that was in him, and it is not strange that he loved it.

In the summer of 1911 his health grew rapidly worse. He went to Byron Hot Springs, California, and later to San Francisco, accompanied by Mrs. Baldwin (who from henceforth was rarely absent from his side) and by his son Dr. William D. Baldwin, in the hope that a change would restore him to at least part of his former strength. Instead he failed gradually and near the end of June, the decision was made to return to the Islands on the steamer Honolulan of the Matson Line. The voyage was made without incident direct to Kahului. As he was carried from the tender to the wharf, he recognized many, including some of the workmen, and called to them cheerily by name. Indeed he was cheery and retained his sense of humor, so far as conscious, until the last. For a little while it was hoped that he would improve, but once arrived at the Maluhia home he lived but a few days and died on July 8, 1911.

Few men have been so honored as he upon their death in so general and spontaneous an expression of grief by all classes of the community. On the afternoon of July 10, the day of the funeral, business was stopped at Honolulu. Many came to Maui from there and from the other Islands on the steamer Mauna Kea, specially chartered for the occasion. No doubt, however, if he had been there to see, the presence and grief of many of the great men of the territory would not have touched his heart as much as the manifestation of grief by the common laborers, who by the hundreds and thousands on foot and horse-back from all over the Island poured into Maluhia and the old church yard at the Makawo Cemetery to do honor to the memory of the man who was employ-er of many and the friend of all, the "Father of Maui" as he was called.

How noble a record he has left to his children and grandchildren! From beginning to end there is no blot on his scutcheon. His success in business came from hard work, energy, constructive imagination, the vision that can see into the future, ability to man-age men and things, common sense, and inflexible honesty. There is nothing here of the craft and the scheming or the ruthlessness one associates with so many of the builders of industry. His was a life of Christianity practically applied. If any one word is significant of his character, perhaps it is justice. Ev-ery man who dealt with him received his due, often more, but never less. When his "worldly task" was done, he might have said with the evangelist:

> I have fought a good fight, I have finished my course, I have kept the faith.